The World Ecotourism Summit

International Year of Ecotourism 2002

World Ecotourism Summit

FINAL REPORT

COMMISSION CANADIENNE DU TOURISME

CANADIAN TOURISM COMMISSION

OMT · WTO · BTO

UNEP

Tourisme Québec

Copyright 2002 World Tourism Organization

World Ecotourism Summit – Final Report

√ **ISBN: 92-844-0550-5**

Published by the World Tourism Organization and the United Nations Environment Programme.
Madrid, Spain

Printed by the World Tourism Organization. Madrid, Spain

Acknowledgements

The World Tourism Organization and the United Nations Environment Programme would like to thank the four experts who were commissioned to prepare the summaries of the regional preparatory meetings and the reports on the different sessions of the World Ecotourism Summit: Ms. Pam Wight (Pam Wight & Associates Tourism Consultants, Canada), Dr. Richard Denman (The Tourism Company, United Kingdom), Mr. Francesc Giró (Fundació Natura, Spain) and Dr. François Vellas (University of Toulouse, France). The comprehensive Final Report was edited by Mr. Richard Denman and revised by Mr. Eugenio Yunis (WTO Chief, Sustainable Development of Tourism Programme, Mr. Gabor Vereczi (WTO, Programme Officer, Sustainable Development of Tourism Section) and Ms. Janine Tabasaran (UNEP, Associate Programme Officer, Tourism Programme).

CONTENTS

1. INTRODUCTION

This report contains the summaries of the debates held and conclusions reached at the World Ecotourism Summit and its preparatory process, as well as the Quebec Declaration on Ecotourism.

The World Ecotourism Summit, was held in Quebec City, Canada from 19 to 22 May, 2002. This was the principal event to mark 2002 as the International Year of Ecotourism.

The Summit was an initiative of the World Tourism Organisation (WTO) and the United Nations Environment Programme (UNEP). It was hosted by Tourisme Québec and the Canadian Tourism Commission. These four organisations were the partners responsible for the Summit.

The purpose of the Summit was to bring together governments, international agencies, NGOs, tourism enterprises, representatives of local and indigenous communities, academic institutions and individuals with an interest in ecotourism, and enable them to learn from each other and identify some agreed principles and priorities for the future development and management of ecotourism.

Main themes

UNEP and WTO, in consultation with other organizations and ecotourism stakeholders, had defined and adopted the following main discussion themes for the International Year of Ecotourism and for the Summit.

Theme A - Ecotourism policy and planning: the sustainability challenge
Sustainable ecotourism plans, policies and programs at international, national and local levels; integration of ecotourism policies into sustainable development plans and frameworks; land use planning; use of natural parks and protected areas; balance between development and conservation objectives in policies; development agency programs on ecotourism and their role in funding related pipeline investments; plans for human resource development in ecotourism.

Theme B - Regulation of ecotourism: institutional responsibilities and frameworks
Legislation, norms and other regulations for ecotourism activities; voluntary schemes and self regulation; certification, accreditation and ecolabels; international and inter-governmental guidelines, principles and codes; roles of different stakeholders in ensuring compliance with regulations or voluntary schemes.

Theme C - Product development, marketing and promotion of ecotourism: fostering sustainable products and consumers
Building sustainable ecotourism products; multistakeholder cooperation for product development especially in protected areas and biosphere reserves; market research, marketing techniques and promotional methods; information to tourists; ethical behaviour; environmental education for consumers; public-private sector relationships for marketing and promotion; co-operative marketing for small ecotourism operations.

Theme D - Monitoring costs and benefits of ecotourism: ensuring equitable distribution among all stakeholders

Measuring economic, ecological and social costs and benefits of ecotourism; contribution to conservation; assessing potential and actual environmental and socio-cultural impacts of ecotourism; taking precautionary measures at local, national, regional and international levels; integrating monitoring and evaluation procedures; research needs and adaptive management systems.

Cross-cutting themes

Throughout the discussions on the four themes the focus was on two main cross-cutting issues:
- The sustainability of ecotourism from the environmental, economic and socio-cultural points of view;
- Involvement and empowerment of local communities and indigenous people in the ecotourism development process, in management and monitoring of ecotourism activities, and in the sharing of benefits resulting from it.

The preparatory process for the Summit

During the latter half of 2001 and the first four months of 2002, 18 preparatory conferences were held. These conferences took place in all the regions of the world, either under the aegis of WTO or of UNEP (in association with The International Ecotourism Society). A list of the conferences can be found later, in the reports of the regional panels. The preparatory conferences provided an opportunity for all kinds of stakeholders in ecotourism to come together to present their experiences and discuss matters of local, regional or international concern. In total over 3,000 delegates attended the conferences and over 300 papers were presented at them.

The preparatory conferences addressed each of the four main themes of the Summit. The combined results of the conferences were summarised in four papers, one for each of the themes, which together formed a discussion paper circulated at the start of the Summit. A copy of this paper can be found in Annex 1.

During April 2002, a web conference was held. This enabled any individual or body, at no cost, to participate in the debate about the four Summit themes. There were 948 registered participants in this conference, a summary of which can be found in Annex 2.

Participants and presentations

A total of 1,169 delegates attended the World Ecotourism Summit, from 132 different countries. The range of delegates included:
- International agencies engaged in supporting conservation, tourism and sustainable development.
- National ministries of tourism, culture and the environment. In total 30 ministers of state attended the Summit.

- Non-governmental organisations working at an international or local level, representing conservation, indigenous communities, travellers and other interests.
- Private sector enterprises engaged directly or indirectly in ecotourism.
- Academics, consultants and other experts in the field of ecotourism.

Registered delegates were invited to submit statements relating to the Summit themes. A total of 180 statement proposals were received. From these, 120 were selected for presentation during the event, considering time limitations of the three-day programme. The selection was based on the relevance and originality of the contribution and on the need to achieve a representative balance of presentations from different types of organisation and parts of the world. In addition to the registered statements, participants had the opportunity to intervene freely throughout the debate sessions.

All statements, whether presented or not, which were received by the deadline were included in a CD-Rom, which was distributed to each delegate. This CD also included the reports from the preparatory conferences.

Structure of the Summit

Following introductory presentations from the partners, the Summit consisted of the following elements:

- A plenary session at which four panels reported on the preparatory conferences held, respectively, in Africa, Asia, the Americas and Europe.
- Four parallel working group sessions, covering the four main themes of the Summit.
- A ministerial forum, and two special forums covering the business perspective and development cooperation in ecotourism.
- A plenary session to receive and debate reports from the four thematic working groups.
- A final plenary session to receive and debate the draft Quebec Declaration on Ecotourism.

The Final Programme of the Summit can be found in Annex 3.

Summit outputs

This report, including the annexes, sets out the issues, key points, recommendations and conclusions arising from the Summit.
The main output from the Summit is the Quebec Declaration on Ecotourism. This has been taken forward to the World Summit on Sustainable Development at Johannesburg, 2002, and has been widely circulated. The full text is included in this report.

The complete text of this report, also the content of the above mentioned CD-Rom, including all statements received and the final reports of the preparatory conferences are available at the following websites:

http://www.ecotourism2002.org
http://www.world-tourism.org/sustainable/IYE-Main-Menu.htm
http://www.uneptie.org/pc/tourism/ecotourism/wes.htm

2. REPORTS FROM THE REGIONAL PANELS

The opportunities presented by ecotourism and the need for its careful management are apparent in all regions of the world. Evidence from the preparatory conferences suggested that the fundamental principles and issues relating to the development of ecotourism are similar in all areas. However, it was also apparent that differences in resources, ecosystems, markets and socio-economic structures, mean that priorities and practicalities vary from region to region.

These similarities and differences were brought out during the reports of the regional panels at the Summit. During each panel session, short presentations were made by selected spokespersons on the preparatory conferences held in that region. In the main, these conferences had focused on the region in which the conference was held, but in a few cases the conferences covered types of destination (e.g. islands, deserts, Arctic lands) irrespective of continent.

Following the presentations on the preparatory conferences, the sessions were opened up to interventions from the floor and a discussion. At the end of each session, the key points that had arisen were identified by the rapporteurs.

Session on preparatory meetings held in Africa

Four reports were presented to the Summit on the preparatory meetings held in the following locations:
- Maputo, Mozambique, March 2001 – for all African states with an emphasis on planning and management
- Nairobi, Kenya, March 2002 – for East Africa
- Mahé, Seychelles, December 2001 – for Small Island Developing States (SIDS) and other Small Islands
- Algiers, Algeria, January 2002 – for Desert Areas

The presentations in this panel demonstrated that ecotourism is one of the main forms of tourism in which Africa has a comparative advantage.

Africa features extensive protected areas hosting a variety of ecosystems and traditional cultures that are major attractions for nature-oriented tourism. In many African countries, vast national and wildlife parks count for many forms of ecotourism activities.

Ecotourism seems the best way to prevent controversial effects and negative impacts on prevailing ecosystems, local communities and traditional cultures and to be a viable source of economic benefits for African countries, if developed and managed in a sustainable manner.

The specific circumstances and needs for different areas were separately identified.

Africa's international comparative advantage: National parks and protected areas

Ecotourism is a great opportunity for African countries and its parks, reserves and protected areas are an international level resource. Thus, many African countries can base their tourism development on exploiting their natural assets on the condition that the rules of sustainable development – the basis of ecotourism – are respected. Conservation of natural resources can become mainstream to socio-economic development in Africa. National parks and reserves in Africa should be considered as a basis for regional development, involving communities living within and adjacent to them. Given their strong international recognition, parks and reserves can be turned to sort of brands, providing advantage in tourism marketing and promotion.

Small islands and coastal zones

Particular attention must be focused on tourism development in small islands as development, even ecotourism development, can be at the origin of environmental and social problems - even before large number of tourist arrivals. This is the case of coastal zones in small islands where ecosystems, notably lagoons, are particularly vulnerable. Appropriate liquid and solid waste treatment systems must be put in place whenever any ecotourism activity is created.

Moreover, ecolabels are particularly important for small insular countries as shown in the example of the Seychelles. Ecolabels can be very useful for achieving landscaping and beautification objectives, such as by encouraging better use of gardens, and for stimulating environmental management, such as energy conservation, waste treatment plants and recycling systems.

Due to the natural and economic specificities of tourism in small islands it is not realistic to focus on ecotourism in the stricter sense. Rather, the broader concept of "sustainable tourism" is often a more effective policy position, though ecotourism plays an important role in further setting the standards for the protection of the natural and cultural environment.

The fragility of island ecosystems must be the cornerstone of any ecotourism plan and any action must respect the island's local, natural and cultural environments.

Desert areas

Desert areas represent comparative and even absolute advantages for Africa, which has the largest desert in the world. Deserts are also some of the largest conservation areas in the world. The seminar in Algiers concluded that there are great opportunities for ecotourism in desert areas – particularly for Africa because of its location near the large tourist generating markets of Europe. Desert areas represent complex ecotourism attractions, showcasing natural, geological, and archaeological features, nomad and other specific cultures and traditions. A special attention should be paid in ecotourism development and management in desert areas to the fragility of ecosystems, the extreme meteorological conditions, the presence of unique archaeological and geological remains, the scarcity of water resources and the difficulties of access.

Importance of trans-boundary cooperation

Many natural zones cross the political borders of several countries and this must be taken into account when developing ecotourism. Indeed, it is impossible to envisage diverging or even opposed development policies in zones shared by several States where there is natural, human and social unity. In this case, trans-boundary cooperation is fundamental for all types of ecotourism development, which implies common policies between countries in the same region. This cooperation is particularly necessary in areas where wildlife crosses administrative and political borders.

The development and management of trans-boundary natural resources and parks has to become a central issue in Africa, recognizing the need to maintain ecological integrity and free movement of wildlife in certain territories that are divided by country frontiers.

The need to find commercial and financial solutions

The commercial viability of ecotourism initiatives is a recurring theme in the debates such as in the case studies presented in the preparatory seminars, specifically in Maputo. Participants emphasised the importance of strengthening small and medium enterprises and particularly micro enterprises to enable them to successfully engage with the tourism industry in Africa. The importance of identifying and demonstrating to funding sources the value of conservation and of ecotourism to national economies in Africa has to be recognised.

The need to reinforce capacity building

There is a lack of awareness of tourism among African local communities. Local communities need to appreciate the benefits and the demerits of tourism. It is important for governments to ensure that communities are trained to administer joint ventures, as without capacity building it is difficult to sustain an equitable approach to management. Capacity building is essential if local communities are to be real stakeholders in the development of ecotourism in Africa.

African necessity to focus on benefits for local people

Speakers and participants identified the need to generate local community benefits from Africa's natural heritage tourism as the critical issue. Ecotourism as a concept has most to offer in the African development context, linking to the rural economy to avoid leakages and maximise local economic benefit from tourism. In Africa, national parks, wildlife reserves and other protected areas have to play a significant role in encouraging local economic development by sourcing food and other locally produced resources.

Session on preparatory meetings held in Asia and the Pacific

Five reports were presented to the Summit on the preparatory meetings held in the following locations:

- New Delhi, India, September 2001 – International NGO Workshop Tourism Towards 2002
- Gangtok, India, January 2002 – Conference for South Asia
- Maldives, February 2002 – Asia-Pacific Ministerial Conference on Sustainable Development of Ecotourism
- Chiang Mai, Thailand, March 2002 – Conference for Southeast Asia
- Fiji, April 2002 – Conference on Sustainable Development of Ecotourism in the South Pacific Islands

The papers and debates from the Session on Asia and the Pacific highlighted a number of issues and perspectives, as follows.

Need for baseline studies

The importance of baseline studies was highlighted, in order to provide a better knowledge on ground conditions, and changes over time. It was recommended that innovative approaches be examined, instead of reliance on government, particularly in under-resourced areas. Suggestions included involving volunteer organisations (e.g., those that provide programmes in which conservation and community development work is combined with educational, cultural exchange and tourist activities), or involving educational institutions (e.g., through PhD students).

Commoditisation in tourism

Particular mention was made of commoditisation in tourism in the region, in large part due to poverty. Commoditisation refers to the degradation of the intrinsic value of cultural items, beliefs, goods, and practices, and may even refer to treating a human being as a good for sale. This trivialisation of culture is demonstrated by the sale of culturally related trinkets, and even by people selling themselves (sexually) to visitors. Organisations developing or managing ecotourism are urged to focus on the improvement of basic human conditions.

Managing Impacts

A range of approaches were mentioned for managing impacts, from pricing and fees, to diversification of product offers (to alleviate crowding). However, a serious impact with no solutions offered, was that of global warming in the region.

The need to integrate a range of perspectives, with communications being key

In some Asia-Pacific destinations, ministries try to push their own agendas on other departments and vice versa (e.g., Tourism and Forestry). This achieves very little except resistance. There needs to be awareness and capacity building in government departments, to understand that ecotourism can be a force to assist both mandates.

It was observed by some participants that some NGOs always feel government actions are wrong, and governments tend to pay less attention to constant criticism. Other participants felt that NGOs have some valid perspectives whether in critique of governments or not, and that NGO comments deserve appropriate attention. It was also felt that some NGOs or governments actually undermine private business. The issue that emerged was: how to integrate the range of perspectives, and how to cooperate to mutually beneficial ends.

Improved communications are required. In particular, it was recommended that:
- governments should establish an open dialogue with local communities, private companies and NGOs;
- governments should develop transparent communication, consultation and decision making processes; and
- public-private partnerships should be seen as a key facilitating mechanism, particularly for informing and educating the travelling public about the consequences of their travels as well as their potential for beneficial action.

Challenges of implementing community participation

The challenge of how to implement sustainability through empowerment and participation was discussed, since local participation has an important role in preserving biodiversity.
- *Bottom-up* participatory processes were recommended (e.g., as in Fiji, where the Fiji Ecotourism Association was formed, so that government and others could more easily communicate with an umbrella industry organisation).
- *Top-down* participatory mechanisms were also recommended, as well as a mechanism for multi-sectoral involvement. It was suggested that communities should be consulted on a range of topics, from product development to elements of marketing.

It was acknowledged that time is required for awareness and capacity building, so that communities are able to participate effectively and make decisions.

Community control of local resources was said to be a key need in the Asia-Pacific region. It was suggested that communities should be involved in all levels of activity, including management.

Participatory management was said to be a key tool in ensuring participation in planning, decision-making and management. An example was given of Sri Lanka, where both poachers and policemen communicate together, and although it has taken five years (as well as time, patience, energy, and the efforts of the Eco-Development Committee), both parties now have confidence in the process, and poachers are using their locally-developed skills in a more sustainable way.

It was agreed that ecotourism is best developed to enhance and complement current community lifestyles and economic activities, rather than basing community economies solely or predominantly on ecotourism, or introducing a completely new activity. It was also frequently stated and agreed that communities should have control over ecotourism, including whether they wanted to have it at all, and if so how much, where, when and of what type.

Human resource development is required

It was recommended that there should be a bigger emphasis on training for local people. In the Asia-Pacific region there is a very great need to incorporate local indigenous peoples into any training programs. It was also felt that communities in general need to have awareness training or information related to ecotourism, and also to be made aware that they may have a choice about tourism or other activities.

A challenge related to this topic was how to develop mechanisms to ensure that revenues from ecotourism activities are invested in training (e.g., on-the-job training, management training, or sending workers to attend conferences).

Regulation and monitoring is required

Regulations can either have a positive role in facilitating movements of tourists and foreign exchange in SE Asia, or can be restrictive. It was suggested that very often poor planning has had adverse consequences and needs to be improved. Also, the lack of enforcement of current regulations is a problem.

Session on preparatory meetings held in The Americas

Six reports were presented to the Summit on the preparatory meetings held in the following locations:

- Cuiabá, Brazil, August 2001, for all American states
- Belize City, Belize, November 2001, for Mesoamerica
- Lima, Peru, February 2002, for the Andean region
- Oaxaca, Mexico, March 2002 – Oaxaca Declaration on Indigenous Tourism
- Buenos Aires, Argentina, April 2002 – First National Conference on Ecotourism
- Web Conference on the Sustainable Development of Ecotourism, April 2002 (http://groups.yahoo.com/group/2002ecotourism/)

The Americas are probably one of the regions in the world where ecotourism is developing fastest. There is also an increasing concern about the involvement of indigenous peoples and local communities both in the planning and development of ecotourism.

The preparatory conference reports showed clearly three main concerns about the development of ecotourism: the involvement of local communities; the need for certification schemes easily accessible to everybody regardless of their economic capacity; and much needed training at all levels. In general, there is consensus about the fact that ecotourism can and is contributing actively to nature conservation in the region, and also to a better quality of life for local people. It has also been recognised that it is very important to learn from past mistakes as well as successes.

Planning

One of the issues raised around planning was the specific problem of trans-boundary areas where there is a need for international regulations. Another important point was that very often not all available scientific information is used for planning.

A further concern was that it is important to have a diverse range of activities besides ecotourism such as agriculture, livestock, forest non-timber products, and others, thus avoiding over-dependence on ecotourism. Shifting from traditional sustainable use of resources (when these uses are sustainable, which is not always the case) to ecotourism is a high-risk strategy for local communities. Besides, in areas where ecotourism products mix with other kinds of tourism, it is agreed that there is a need to increase the sustainability of all tourism products.

Regulation and certification

A suitable approach regarding regulation is to follow a process leading from optional guidelines to obligatory regulations. Codes of conduct need to be established as well as procedures and all stakeholders should adopt these. The importance of ethics among operators, the community and consumers was also identified as one of the key issues.

Another important point raised was that regulation of ecotourism needs stakeholders sharing a similar concept of ecotourism.

It was agreed that there is a need for more transparency in certification processes and that these should relate both to environmental aspects as well as quality and participation of local communities. International certification systems are believed to be too expensive and it was suggested that local initiatives should be recognised by international systems. It was suggested that certification should occur at different levels that are more suited to specific regional and local conditions and allow community-based companies to take part in the process. There were proposals to establish incentives for certified companies. Finally it was recognised that in some areas there is a risk of a proliferation of eco-labels.

Participation of indigenous and local people

One of the main concerns was the lack of public participation in the process of planning for ecotourism in many places. It was stressed that local communities need to be the main actors and that they must take part not only in the planning process but also in the management of ecotourism products, which generally means also taking risks. A particularly sensitive issue was the concern among indigenous people about the fact that in some of their lands ecotourism development is being imposed by governments and private companies, without proper consultation and participation.

Capacity building and training

Capacity building and training were identified as key points in the proper development of ecotourism in the region. This included the need for capacity building of local communities, training and technical support. An important point raised was that training needs to be realistic, not creating too high expectations for local communities.

Policy makers were also identified as important targets for training and it was shown that they need to learn about ecotourism in the field. Very often policies are in the hands of people with very little practical experience in the subject. Another target much in need of education about ecotourism is the media in general, who very often cover ecotourism but without reflecting properly its real essence.

Marketing

A fairly common problem in the Americas is that marketing generally focuses in landscape, wildlife and cultural issues and does not put enough emphasis in social, environmental and sustainability aspects, which should be part of responsible marketing communications and very often can be of interest to potential visitors.

In recent years there has been a great development of communications within the region and the Internet has become an important tool for marketing, even for small companies and communities, as well as in remote areas where Cybercafés can be accessible. The Internet can fulfil its potential only if capacity-building and access to modern technology is provided in order to empower ecotourism stakeholders for the adequate use of this media.

Session on preparatory meetings held in Europe

Four reports were presented to the Summit on the preparatory meetings held in the following locations:
- St. Johann / Pongau and Werfenweng, Salzburg, Austria 12-15 September 2001 – for mountain areas, with an emphasis on European ecotourism
- Almaty, Kazakhstan, 17-18 October 2001 – for the transitional economies of the CIS countries, Mongolia and China
- Thessaloniki, Greece, 2-4 November 2001 – for European, Middle East and Mediterranean countries
- Hemavan, Sweden, April 2002 – for the Arctic countries, including North America and Asia as well as Europe

In addition, a paper was presented by the Minister of Tourism of Turkey.

Although the term 'ecotourism' is less frequently used in Europe than in other continents, the presentations showed that the principles and concepts associated with it are equally important here as elsewhere. Europe has many wilderness areas, yet in much of the continent attractive rural landscapes and biodiversity are dependent on traditional land management practices. There is increasing recognition within Europe of the important and mutually supporting relationship between tourism, agriculture, viable rural communities and the conservation of nature.

The preparatory conference reports demonstrated the contrasts to be found within Europe, in terms of landscapes, climate, culture and management priorities. The specific circumstances and needs of different areas were separately identified.

Mountains

Mountains are important locations for ecotourism. The report from the conference in Austria recognised the important linkages between the objectives of the International Year of Mountains and the International Year of Ecotourism, both declared for 2002 by the UN. Mountainous areas often display a particular cultural richness, economic fragility, a decline in traditional populations and activities, and sensitive biodiversity. Mountain communities can use ecotourism to address these issues. There is a close relationship between the needs and opportunities of ecotourism and sustainable activity tourism in mountains.

The Mediterranean

This area receives some of the largest volumes of tourist arrivals in the world, concentrated on the coastal belt. Yet, this is an area of rich biodiversity and also has immense cultural resources. The report from the conference in Greece identified the opportunity for ecotourism in the coastal hinterland and more remote inland areas, as a way of improving the image of Mediterranean destinations, diversifying the offer, reducing seasonality and bringing economic benefits to areas suffering depopulation. Careful planning will be essential.

The CIS countries

These countries have extensive natural areas including forests, wetlands, plains and mountains. Potential for ecotourism is considerable. However, as economies and societies in transition they have particular needs, especially in terms of the general services and infrastructure for tourism. Important issues include clarifying national objectives for ecotourism, stimulating and catering for the domestic market, filling knowledge gaps, easing visa restrictions and promoting cross-border cooperation.

The Arctic

This is a sensitive area with its own particular needs. The traditional values and practices of the indigenous peoples of the Arctic, in protecting and using natural resources, should be recognised, as should their rights over land and water. The report from the conference held in Sweden identified the need for certification programmes for ecotourism which take account of the particular circumstances of the Arctic. Appropriate codes of conduct for visitors and operators need to be applied. A restructuring of the cruise ship licensing system was called for, with local people having control over the use of their areas for ecotourism.

In addition to these priorities relating to specific areas or ecosystems, a number of general themes of particular importance in the European context can be identified from the presentations and the subsequent discussion.

Taking an integrated approach to destination planning

There is strong recognition in Europe of the need for a holistic approach to the planning and development of destinations for sustainable tourism, both in terms of providing a quality experience for visitors and addressing all the impacts of tourism. Ecotourism should be seen within this context. There should be concern about physical infrastructure, destination marketing and information services, linkages with other economic sectors, and relationships with other forms of tourism.

The important role of local authorities in supporting the development and management of sustainable tourism, including ecotourism, is well understood in Europe. This is helped by well-established local democratic structures, effective land use planning and development control processes. At the same time, the need to foster a participative approach at a local level, for example through engaging village communities, is recognised.

Addressing transport and other access issues

The use of transport to, and within, the destination was a key concern of the preparatory conference in Austria. Where possible, ecotourism should be based on forms of mobility which have low environmental impact. Discussion at the Summit widened the debate on access, with a call for more attention to be paid to facilitating access to rural and natural areas, including mountains, for example through networks of hiking trails.

Being concerned about demand and equity amongst users

Demand management was felt to be an important issue in the European context. Points made about this during the discussion included:
- avoiding discrimination and increasing access to ecotourism experiences for people with disabilities and disadvantages;
- promoting opportunities to domestic visitors, ensuring that they are not put off by high prices (e.g. in the CIS countries); and
- influencing larger tour operators as well as more specialist operators (e.g. in the Mediterranean).

Showing responsibility in promoting ecotourism in less developed countries

Europe is a source region for much global ecotourism. The responsibility of European governments and operators in encouraging more sustainable forms of ecotourism, and in providing technical advice and support in this field, is recognised.

3. REPORTS FROM THE THEMATIC WORKING GROUPS

The second full day of the Summit was devoted to four separate working groups on
the four Summit themes.

Each working group meeting started with the presentation of a report from an expert,
appointed by WTO and UNEP, which summarised the results of the preparatory
conferences and served as discussion paper for the Summit concerning the theme in
question. These reports are reproduced in Annex 1.

A total of 71 presentations were made to the four working groups. These were
restricted in time, to enable a range of topics to be covered and to give as many people
as possible a chance to speak. Two presentations from the host country, Canada, were
made during the first session of each group. The presentations were grouped into four
sessions throughout the day, and after each one at least half an hour was allowed for
interventions from the floor and for debate. In the closing session, the WTO/UNEP
╌ts summed up the main points to be taken forward to the final day of the
╌ these were further discussed and expanded by delegates during a final

ort from each working group was made to a full
This was followed by a discussion period which
ance to make further points about each theme, and to
working groups.

set out the issues discussed and the key points and
the working groups, while also taking account of the
session.

mmary reports of the preparatory conferences, adding to,
points made in them. A short resume of the key points
conferences is given, before the points arising from the
ence should be made to Annex 1 for the full coverage.

were repeated in more than one workshop. This is inevitable
of ecotourism relate to all of the themes and each of the
For example, ecotourism planning needs to take account of
regulation issues, and vice versa.

Working group – A

ECOTOURISM POLICY AND PLANNING:
The sustainability challenge

Ecotourism is a complex activity, often seeking to meet a range of objectives, involving a variety of stakeholders and taking place in environmentally and economically fragile locations. It therefore needs careful planning. This working group was concerned with the frameworks, structures and processes of ecotourism planning and policy-making to maximise sustainability and local benefit.

There were eighteen presentations to the working group, which covered:
- National ecotourism planning, policy-making and strategy development – Botswana, Chile, Cote d'Ivoire, Haiti, Rwanda, France, Brazil, Senegal, Tanzania, the Mayan World
- Ecotourism planning systems in federal and provincial parks – Canada
- A case study of ecosystem changes in tourist destinations – Nepal
- Guidelines to minimise negative impacts of ecotourism in vulnerable ecosystems (the Convention on Biological Diversity) or small islands (Seychelles)
- Integrated planning and management in rural areas – Greece, Chile
- Policies developed by origin countries for minimising tourism impacts in destinations – The Netherlands

1. ISSUES DISCUSSED

The main issues discussed were:

- The best structures and tools for effective ecotourism planning, which relate to all objectives
- Planning for environmental conservation
- Planning for economic development
- Gaining social and cultural benefits
- Multi-stakeholder participation

The following specific issues arose throughout the debates:

The relationship between ecotourism and sustainable tourism

It was suggested that planning and policy development for sustainable tourism was the appropriate context for ecotourism planning, since ecotourism embraces the principles of sustainable tourism concerning the economic, social and environmental impacts of tourism. On the other hand, it was also suggested that there was merit in highlighting the particular characteristics of ecotourism, bringing positive benefits for conservation and communities and not simply avoiding negative impacts. It was recognised that ecotourism products may vary considerably, but that all should adhere to basic ecotourism principles.

Lack of appropriate infrastructure and services in destinations

In many destinations with ecotourism potential, it is felt that there is a lack of infrastructure (e.g., accommodation) and services (e.g., well-trained guides).

Foreign ownership or low levels of local jobs minimise local benefits

The issue of foreign ownership draining many of the benefits at the local level was raised. This is particularly the case with respect to infrastructure. In addition, the level and quality of jobs in which local people are employed is too often inadequate (e.g., in Senegal).

Ecotourism brand

The themes of the Summit are in many cases strongly interrelated. Within the Planning and Policy Development sessions, there were discussions about the desire to prevent the use of the word ecotourism by those who do not adhere to its principles, through some type of trademark or branding protection, although the difficulties in this were also acknowledged. This whole topic was the focus of considerable discussion in Session B, and reference to that section provides further insight.

Uncontrolled penetration of ecotourism activities into new areas

The penetration of ecotourism (or other forms of tourism) to remote areas can create management and monitoring problems. For example, in Egypt treks go to very remote areas of the country, which are mostly desert. The difficulty of monitoring tourism operations in remote areas enables the stealing of artefacts, fossils, etc.

2. KEY POINTS AND RECOMMENDATIONS

A number of key points and recommendations arising from the working group were specifically related to conservation, economic development, social benefits and stakeholder participation. However, there were many points that cut across these issues and these are presented first.

Key crosscutting recommendations

Main recommendations from the preparatory conferences:
- Integrate ecotourism policies and planning across national boundaries
- Ensure national governments provide necessary leadership and guidance
- Create a planning framework for protected areas
- Formulate ecotourism plans jointly between public agencies, NGOs and other stakeholders, with a long term vision and clear goals
- Develop tools to assist in planning and management of ecotourism (e.g. appropriate land use planning and visitor management techniques)

- Provide adequate and appropriate funding for projects, protected areas and partnerships
- Involve governments, development agencies, NGOs, private businesses and others in building local capacity, to encourage participation and employment of local people
- Ensure careful consultation and participation of all stakeholders in planning and policy development processes.

Key points arising from the Summit:

Using transboundary management approaches

The need for trans-national policies was emphasised, related to many aspects of tourism, such as easier movement of peoples between regions, and cooperation with respect to shared ecosystem management.

Humans should be recognised and acknowledged as being a *part* of the ecosystem (as opposed to only *using* ecosystems). Transboundary movement possibilities should be built into plans and policies.

There was a recommendation that a world fund be established to enable appropriate ecotourism development particularly at the trans-national level, with the focus intended to be on enhancing cooperative activities between jurisdictions. However, no specific proposal was made on the nature and source of the fund.

It was proposed that global regions (e.g., the Caribbean) should come together for a range of planning and policy development functions (e.g., to highlight issues which have regional relevance).

Taking a collaborative approach to planning and policy development

There should be an overall national vision of how ecotourism can serve biodiversity, as well as how biodiversity can serve ecotourism. One of the biggest problems is lack of a sectoral planning perspective (e.g., the frequent divorce in dialogue between tourism agencies and environmental agencies). All agencies need to work together. It is recommended that lessons and failures be taken from such planning processes as Integrated Coastal Zone Management Studies, for integrating ecotourism planning. Integrated planning should be actively pursued, including collaboration with stakeholders.

Government must take a holistic perspective when developing sustainability strategies, which is both spatial and sectoral (e.g., as in Greece). Ecotourism planning should be conducted within the context of sustainable tourism planning, which in turn should relate to the wider context of planning for sustainable development. Ecotourism planning, actions and policies should be developed with the knowledge that they are likely to be applicable to other forms of tourism, and in all likelihood will be a force for positive change throughout tourism, considering the trends towards mainstreaming ecotourism values and principles. For example, in Tanzania, there are major policy reforms stimulated by the International Year of Ecotourism, which are focussing on poverty reduction through a range of sectoral perspectives such as developing economic opportunities and empowering communities through community participation.

Sectoral integration should be a foundation of all planning and policy development (not only in ecotourism). For example, Chile's National Action Plan is based on an integrated approach, and has been done with the private sector, in a bottom-up manner. Another example is found in the Seychelles, where there are not only various topical themes within their National Environmental Management Plan (including tourism and aesthetics), but there are significant cross-cutting themes (education, awareness and advocacy; partnerships, public consultation and civil society participation; training and capacity-building; management; science, research and technology; monitoring and assessment; vulnerability and global climate change).

It was recommended that whatever the mechanisms, all decision-making be transparent, and also accountable.

Developing appropriate tools for planning and management

It was recommended that appropriate scale in ecotourism development be a part of planning considerations. For example, some destinations build in development controls ahead of time (e.g., Botswana has, as part of its planning framework, deliberately stipulated small-sizes for their ecolodges and camps, or temporary facility structures to enable them to be moved in the future).

There was a comment that in many areas, policies and regulations may exist, but are not implemented. While appropriate planning and policy development is one requirement, rigorous implementation is fundamental.

Planning systematically for protected areas

It was emphasised in debates that a protected area system must form a key part of planning and policy making for ecotourism, and that protected area managers be involved in planning initiatives (not only senior government officials).

A severe problem for protecting biodiversity and protected areas was felt to be the fragmentation of ecosystems. It was recommended that the issue of adequate size of protected areas be addressed in development and planning. It was suggested that a useful educational and management tool is the creation of maps to illustrate locations, threats, or other spatial variables, so indicating where it is most necessary to conserve biodiversity.

Committing adequate financial and other resources

Some countries lack the ability to mobilize the resources necessary to address significant ecotourism planning and policy development needs. Multilateral aid is required in the form of various types of assistance. One recommendation was that there be support for centres of development and dissemination of knowledge and cooperation; another was that there be a fund for trans-national ecotourism development.

The public may be encouraged to contribute funds. It was suggested that visitors and others should be able to donate funds to projects, and should receive some recognitions and benefits which reinforce the value of their donation. For example, the Coral Reef Action Network offers donors a range of educational reminders: stickers to heighten awareness, CD with a tool kit for customers, wall calendar, passport, poster, boaters' chart, quiz and similar items. These educate and keep donors involved with the project. In addition, they give donors guarantees that all their contributions will go to the chosen project.

It was suggested that some funding for education, in schools and elsewhere, be set aside from ecotourism revenues.

Capacity building

Training and capacity building is required for those professionals who are involved in planning and policy development. It is recommended that the WTO and other international institutions support or fund programs which train public officials who will be planning and developing policies, in order to build capacity within ministries and similar institutions (e.g., this could be through national level training institutions). This suggestion of appropriate training was also made for the personnel of park and protected area authorities.

At a more local level, it was suggested that the WTO and other institutions should continue to expand training programs, such as for local authorities, indigenous people and other stakeholders. Another suggestion was that a range of types of support be examined to develop capabilities locally, such as guiding skills.

It was recommended that tour operators also be involved in education and training.

Education and awareness-building is recommended as a significant tool for all players, from lodge owners and tour operators to local communities and young people. Suggestions included such innovative ideas as developing education caravans for community awareness building, or creating coursework for schools to better understand the concept of impact.

The views and perspectives of youth are a key influence on positive future directions. It is recommended that sustainable tourism education of young people be built into educational programs and ministry curricula in all countries.

It was recommended that the Internet be better used for information exchange. International agencies should collaborate to compile a database of information, which is web accessible, continually updated, and includes information on best practice for sustainable tourism and for ecotourism. It was suggested that qualified websites with useful information should be able to link to this site.

Building multi-stakeholder participation into policy and planning processes

Mechanisms should be developed to include a range of stakeholders in planning and policy development. It is always easier for governments to deal with umbrella organisations than with operators directly, thus developing industry organisations may assist. For example, Parks Canada and the Tourism Industry Association of Canada have developed an accord concerning heritage-based tourism, which is currently focussed on agreement about principles, which acknowledge shared stewardship in managing and protecting national heritage places.

Indigenous peoples' representatives (e.g., Shushwap Nation, in Canada) emphasised the need to build targeted participative mechanisms into planning and policy development. Since indigenous peoples tend not only to be the poorest members of society, but also to have land based economies and cultures (involving hunting, fishing and gathering), it is critical to involve them early in any processes.

Other suggestions for including stakeholder participation came from Tourism Quebec, who suggests that integrated management requires that there be government centres close and accessible to citizens (decentralised communications points).

It was also emphasised that past experience should be brought into the planning and policy development processes (e.g., South Africa) so that there is greater integration of ecotourism activities into the way of life of communities. It was recommended that the Global Code of Ethics developed by the WTO should be adopted by all stakeholders, to promote a balanced perspective in different forms of tourism development, including ecotourism.

It was also agreed that ecotourism should not be developed if consultation revealed that local communities did not want to have it.

Recommendations for Environmental Conservation

Main recommendations from the preparatory conferences:
- Conserve energy, water, and other resources, reduce waste and favour materials that are not imported.
- Plan more sustainable transport options.
- Promote awareness of conservation and biodiversity amongst local people and visitors.
- Use appropriate tools to identify limits to use and to manage impacts.
- Seek to influence demand as well as managing visitors who do come.
- Use economic tools, information and interpretation in visitor management.

Key points arising from the Summit:

Educating communities about biodiversity and conservation

It was felt that many local communities did not understand the value of biodiversity very well, and that education was needed. Visitors should also be educated about the value of biodiversity and that natural resources belong to local peoples and should not be removed by visitors (souveniring, biopiracy, or removal of fossils, etc.).

Managing impacts

Primarily, it is essential to ensure that ecotourism does not have negative impacts, and that operations adopt minimum impact practices and guidelines (e.g., in the St Laurent or Yukon areas of Canada). Other options are planning in the destination to *exclude* certain activities (e.g., in the Seychelles, where there are certain banned activities). In some locations, government regulations are required (e.g., to ensure that cruise ships adhere to minimum environmental standards where ships do not take voluntary action).

It is recommended that management decision-making be built into plans, together with other techniques (such as forecasting, environmental and social impact assessments or monitoring), to address potential problems or impacts as a preventative measure.

Managing visitors

Overall, it was recommended that an integrated approach is applied for the management of many variables, including supply and demand. Supply considerations, such as resources or culture, should be of primary concern, but management should also take full account of markets and demand.

Recommendations for Economic Development

Main recommendations from the preparatory conferences:
• Provide training, micro-credit and other assistance to small, medium and micro-enterprises.
• Provide incentives for enterprises to pursue sustainability
• Provide infrastructure, such as access and telecommunications, to assist communities in ecotourism development.
• Emphasise the role of governments as facilitators rather than operators.
• Place an emphasis on increasing retained economic value per visitor rather than expanding visitor volumes.

Key points arising from the Summit:

Providing government and other support for community level ecotourism

It was confirmed that the state should be a partner, *not* a developer of ecotourism operations.

In recognition that there is a spectrum of market interests, and a spectrum of tourism opportunities, there may be scope to link nature to cultural tourism and even to mass tourism (e.g., in Greece) particularly in areas where there are fewer pristine environments, in order to heighten the attraction of the destinations, and to generate community benefits.

Communities need a source of funds which can be linked to development. There may be opportunities to create community institutions and link them to forms of income generation; or to create Community Conservation Funds for donors, so ecotourism is viewed as a business by communities.

International assistance should be targeted more towards ecotourism projects. Assistance can be given in the form of finance, technology, training, information, mentorship, or in other ways. Loans might be given to countries, for example for training. Assistance could be targeted and conditional upon performance (e.g., demonstrating environmental protection). It is recommended that international agencies coordinate sources and conditions of assistance, and provide centralised and up to date information (e.g., on a website) for easy access by needy destinations.

Other forms of assistance may include staffing and human resources, and volunteer labour. This can provide a sense of ownership of the project by participants (e.g., in Senegal there are agreements between Parks and volunteers).

Recognising mutual benefits

Often, there are contributions which local communities bring to ecotourism or other developments, which are not viewed in terms of having conventional value (e.g., in Uganda, these might be spiritual, medicinal, or other information or cultural activities). It was felt that while ecotourism development can bring value to local communities, at the same time local communities can contribute valuable knowledge and information, practices, traditions, etc. to agencies, entrepreneurs, visitors, or others. In some cases, local people provide such information or knowledge without any recompense or benefit. It was recommended that such local contributions and sharing should be valued through financial or similar means. In this way there is likely to be more understanding that contributions are *mutual*, rather than the view that benefit flows are uni-directional to communities.

Exchanges of information can be of equal value to communities and to planners and policy makers. For example, imported technologies must be appropriate to the communities. However, indigenous technologies must also be acknowledged (such as India's Care and Share program), since traditional ecological and other knowledge and technologies will also have great value. For example, the Austrian Parliament has just called for a respect for the knowledge of indigenous peoples as a basis for sustainable development, and for indigenous land rights as a basis for human rights.

Recommendations for Social and Cultural Benefits

Main recommendations from the preparatory conferences:
- Use historic buildings and other heritage resources, thereby contributing to their protection.

- Involve communities in social and cultural programmes, to ensure   local control, ownership and authenticity.
- Mount community awareness campaigns.
- Ensure that tour operators and other external companies are aware of their responsibilities towards communities.

Key points arising from the Summit:

Involving communities and ensuring local ownership

A number of areas have problems due to overpopulation (e.g., European coastal areas) while other areas (e.g., mountains) may suffer from depopulation. It was suggested that ecotourism may provide some benefits to both areas, by alleviating pressures on the coast, while attracting visitors (and development) to rural areas. For example, in Greece the planning process aims to link natural areas with cultural tourism and to link these to mass tourism destinations.

It is recommended that governments consider providing communities with land or resources which can enable them to act as partners in ecotourism operations. Botswana has allocated wildlife management areas to local communities for consumptive or non-consumptive use in tourism, so they can share in ecotourism benefits. An additional benefit is that this has led to decreased poaching.

Communities should have input to planning processes through, for example, local narratives and guides, wherein they provide information to visitors, plus develop their own self-esteem.

Communities should be involved and empowered, such that there is *no* ecotourism development where there is no desire for involvement in tourism. Opportunities should be sought to build on current economic and community activities rather than developing some totally new product.

Recommendations for multi-stakeholder participation

Main recommendations from the preparatory conferences:
- Build support for joint ventures into planning and policy initiatives
- Facilitate community-level joint ventures, such as co-management of protected areas
- Encourage strategic alliances between private businesses and local communities.

Key points arising from the Summit

Encouraging joint ventures

Origin-destination joint ventures were suggested. One innovative example is in the Netherlands, where there is increasing awareness by tourists or tour operators that they may be the source of problems when they visit other destinations. An outgoing tourism policy has been developed, and moves to link outgoing tourism with NGOs in receiving destinations.

It was emphasised by Tanzania that there needs to be strong involvement by the private sector in partnerships, not just governments or NGOs. The Tanzanian delegation to the Summit included a great many industry representatives as well as government representatives.

Overall, throughout the discussions on policy and planning, the points made at the preparatory conferences were reinforced, with the topics summarised above being the main focus of discussion. In addition, it was also said that the International Year of Ecotourism has already stimulated some of the actions and directions identified above.

Working Group – B

THE REGULATION OF ECOTOURISM:
Institutional responsibilities and frameworks

The impacts of ecotourism on society and the environment can be positive and negative. The theme addressed by this working group was about providing the right regulatory frameworks and systems to ensure that products that are developed and marketed as ecotourism are beneficial and not harmful to environments and communities.

Nineteen presentations were made to the working group, covering:
• Examples of regulation and control of ecotourism - Quebec, Mexico, Japan and Seychelles.
• Certification systems – The experiences of existing and planned new certification schemes in Australia, Peru, and Costa Rica as well as the examples from the USA and Europe.
• International guidelines for ecotourism – Austria, Germany and Europarc.
• The need for quality control and for the identification of indicators – emphasised in two Canadian presentations.
• Specific methodologies and practical examples, from Uruguay, Indonesia, India and Korea.
• Ecotourism and ethics, presented by the representative of The Vatican.

1. ISSUES DISCUSSED

The following were the main issues discussed by the working group.

Institutional frameworks

Legal frameworks and regulations are not always established for ecotourism only and very often are common to other kinds of tourism. The need to have specific legal frameworks and policies for ecotourism was stressed by different speakers, although in some cases it has proved difficult to have the same framework in different regions of a single country.

In some cases the work of individual countries is not enough to guarantee that ecotourism is properly developed. There were proposals in the Korean presentation to promote action for ecotourism development at the international level.

The need to develop ecotourism strategies at the national level through a consultation process was well demonstrated in the Seychelles.

Regulation of Ecotourism

The role of the private sector in the establishment of regulations and in the certification process was discussed and different viewpoints were expressed. While some people felt that the private sector should take part in defining regulations, others considered that governments and NGOs should establish regulations in order to guarantee the preservation of natural and cultural resources.

Certification and labelling

These were issues that brought a number of questions and discussions. One of the points was whether certification should be just a voluntary process, or whether it should be an instrument to complement the regulation of ecotourism ventures. Another important point raised by different people concerned the components of certification schemes. Other aspects, beyond environmental issues, need to be taken into account and included.

The scale of certification met with a great deal of interest. How can certification schemes work at the local level and at the same time have international recognition? In relation to this, how to cover the cost of certification at the local level was a big concern in many areas and proposals were made to overcome this problem so that it can be made accessible to all sizes of business as well as to local communities. In Peru , for example, some communities receive technical and financial support from academic bodies, while in Australia, the cost of certification is proportional to the size of the business.

A final point discussed is the problem of the appearance of pseudo-eco-labels: too many labels are confusing and there was agreement that something should be done in this respect. A possible solution is the example of VISIT, a joint European initiative for the promotion of ecolabels and sustainable tourism development. VISIT has co-operated with 10 leading ecolabels in Europe and developed common basic standards for their criteria and verification procedures. These standards allow the identification of those ecolabels which guarantee a high environmental quality of their certified hotels, campsites, beaches or marinas. In 2004, VISIT will be established as a European accreditation body for ecolabels in tourism.

Sustainability indicators and monitoring

The need to monitor sustainability of ecotourism products was discussed and a number of approaches were presented. The difficulty of identifying indicators for social and cultural aspects was pointed out. Surveys to determine visitor satisfaction could be used to evaluate the quality of the visitor experience. At the same time, local people should be made aware of what was being done to the environment and how this would affect them.

A good example was the "European Charter for Sustainable Tourism in Protected Areas" which has proved to be a valuable tool for ensuring that tourism in protected areas is managed according to the principles of sustainable development.

Capacity building, training and education

This was considered a key issue for the sustainable development of ecotourism. Without adequate training and education of all stakeholders, from government to the private sector and consumers, in matters relating to regulation, certification and monitoring, it is impossible to progress towards sustainability in ecotourism. All players need to understand why some sort of regulation is necessary in many situations, why certification can help both the business and the environment, and finally why monitoring is essential to demonstrate that progress is being made towards sustainability.

Other issues

The impact of transport in relation to ecotourism was a key point in some of the discussions and suggestions were made on how to take it into account in ecotourism products and in certification schemes.

2. KEY POINTS AND RECOMMENDATIONS

Institutional frameworks

Main recommendations from the preparatory conferences:
- Ensure coordination between government ministries in the planning and regulation of ecotourism.

- Develop a framework of cooperation between public, private and non-governmental organisations.
- Ensure institutions understand the different dimensions of sustainable tourism and ecotourism.

Key points arising from the Summit:

There is a need to reach agreements between protected area management bodies, tourism departments or ministries as well as the tourism industry in general. A good example of this is the progress being made by the Canadian certification program. Good coordination among protected area managers and tourism departments is extremely important.

The development of legislative frameworks at the regional level should be supported, because they can positively influence sustainability issues, including the promotion of ecotourism and similar types of tourism harmonized with the environment. The recent establishment of quality and specifically ecotourism product rules in Québec, Canada, is a promising example in this field.

Incentives should be set up, such as lower taxes or public land concessions at lower rates, for ecotourism operators that promote environmentally-sensitive land use (e.g., the ones working on Crown land in British Columbia, Canada). At the same time, in Ontario, Canada, regulatory requirements ensure that resource stewardship agreements are established between the State and tour operators working within an area covered by the agreement, to preserve natural areas of high tourism value. This approach reserves the most pristine areas for ecotourism operations. The idea, in both examples, is to stimulate proper ecotourism in sensitive and valuable natural areas with a high potential.

Regulation of ecotourism

Main recommendations from the preparatory conferences:
- Move gradually from optional guidelines and simple codes of conduct towards obligatory regulations.
- Establish suitable legal frameworks underpinned by effective tools for regulating ecotourism.
- Develop guidelines and best practice information at all levels.
- Ensure protected areas are consulted and involved in regulatory procedures.

Key points arising from the Summit:

Tourism operators, local government, and conservation departments should establish regulations. They should guarantee the protection of sensitive natural resources and cultural integrity.

Legislation and regulations should be specific for ecotourism A good example was the case study of Tourisme Quebec where a very specific legal framework is being established, clearly separating adventure tourism activities and ecotourism with an objective of avoiding a severe impact upon natural assets.

In some areas regulations need to be compulsory since in many countries voluntary regulations do not work and very often the public asks for minimum obligatory regulations, as it was presented in the example from Mexico.

Certain laws and regulations within protected areas should be extended beyond their frontiers.

Legally binding instruments for the implementation of sustainable ecotourism and avoidance of non-sustainable forms of tourism for sensitive areas should be established.

Strict regulations for ecotourism at an international level should be avoided, while guidelines are acceptable.

The potential negative impact of visitors should be taken into account from the beginning of the planning process. This can be realised through some measures such as reservation systems, routing in sensitive points, zoning within the site according to carrying capacity. The Bodogol Education Center, in Indonesia, has successfully put in place some of these preventive measures.

Certification

Main recommendations from the preparatory conferences:
- Provide guidelines on certification schemes for ecotourism.
- Avoid penalise very small scale enterprises and facilitate their access to certification schemes.
- Involve all stakeholders in developing and implementing certification processes.
- Ensure certification processes are transparent, understandable and updated.

Key points arising from the Summit:

Certification processes need to be global in concept, following international guidelines and recommendations, but local in application. An example of this is the need for ecolodge guidelines, which can always be adopted at the local level and can then be followed by some sort of international ecolodge certification.

Auditing teams must be independent and ideally should have representatives from different countries and proper training. They should also have different cultural backgrounds.

Certification should take into account social, economic and cultural aspects, besides the environmental ones. Most of the existing concepts for eco-labels, brands and certification systems have to be enlarged by social and cultural aspects to reach the aims of sustainable ecotourism.

NGOs should take part in the process of identifying certification schemes. In many cases NGOs have developed voluntary certification schemes which have afterwards been regulated and spread by governments.

International certification schemes must be multistakeholder. They should be promoted by international organizations including governments, academia, conservation NGOs, the private sector and with proper consultation with local and indigenous people. It was suggested that organizations such as WTO and UNEP could play a role in establishing an international framework for tourism certification systems and all existing certification schemes should be considered in this process.

Certification and accreditation should be industry driven and paid for by the operators, as they can use it as a marketing tool and possibly marketing advantage over competitors, therefore it can be beneficial and profitable. The case of Australia is particularly interesting with well-established ecotourism and ecoguides certification programs.

In the case of very small businesses in developing countries, there should be technical and financial support through grant or loans or micro-credit systems to assist in making the necessary changes and to cover the costs of certification, either from strong NGOs, local government, academic bodies, larger profitable businesses or development agencies. There was agreement that environmental certification very often leads to economic benefits since energy, water and other resources are saved.

Easily accessible funding formulae to cover the cost of international certification schemes should be explored, so that small businesses can have access to them. Other funding and capacity building mechanisms should be identified and promoted for this purpose.

Ecotourism certifiers must be guided by social criteria geared to facilitating the integration of small businesses at preferential rates and through technical contributions or the promotion of collective certification alternatives.

Financially sound NGOs should shoulder the role of a certification body at a cost more affordable for local entrepreneurs.

Certification should provide powerful incentives and guidelines for responsible business practices.

A multistakeholder Sustainable Tourism Stewardship Council, such as the one being considered by Rainforest Alliance in coordination with a range of international organizations, could help local certification programs exchange information in a forum that allows for accreditation of certifiers, marketing and credibility.

The obligatory introduction of certification systems for ecotourism facilities and operations should be considered at least at regional and national levels, to guarantee that the quality provided is consistent with the principles of sustainability. This is the case of the national ecocertification scheme which will become compulsory in the near future in the Seychelles.

Capacity building, training and education

Key points arising from the Summit:

In the certification process, there is a need to train and educate all stakeholders, including the industry, operators and customers or consumers. This latter case is particularly important since the interest of consumers in true ecotourism will reward good products and punish examples of "greenwashing". A good example of consumer education is the brochure "Your Travel Choice Makes a Difference" from The International Ecotourism Society.

Certification programs should be promoted and explained to the public by both the tourism and the environmental authorities.

Education, transfer of know how, exchange and respect for local people must drive the development of ecotourism in all destinations. In the long term, customers will reward or punish ecotourism products according to their sustainability.

Demand from consumers and tour operators is a prerequisite for a certification system to work. Tourists must be informed of certification schemes and therefore, the promotion by government (by both the environment and tourist departments) is essential.

Monitoring and indicators

Main recommendations from the preparatory conferences:
- Include the economic, social and environmental impact of tourism in monitoring.
- Define targets to be achieved in a certain period of time.
- Establish continuous data collection, involving businesses and tourists.
- Ensure monitoring is a prerequisite of providing assistance to projects.

Key points arising from the Summit:

The issue of monitoring and indicators was central to the discussions of Working Group D, but the following specific points were raised within this working group.

The definition of sustainability indicators should not be left only to the private sector and should be the result of consensus among all stakeholders including local people, NGOs, government and protected area managers.

Sustainability indicators should be integrated with local planning.

Indicators must be identified at the local level and should take into account environmental, social and cultural factors.

New methods of evaluation of progress towards sustainability in ecotourism need to be identified, that are accessible to the local population both from the technical and economic point of view.

Other recommendations

It was suggested that World Ecotourism Sites should be declared, where ecotourism would be promoted by the international community in order to guarantee the conservation of high value natural resources and the well being of local people.

Travellers should be made aware of their environmental impact due to transport and its effect on global warming when travelling to remote destinations. The impact of transport in ecotourism has not received enough attention.

Travellers should receive information on positive and relatively simple ways to compensate for their impact, such as taking part in reforestation projects in the areas visited.

The three pillars of sustainable development -public welfare, economy and environment- have to be effectively built into ecotourism.

The development and management of sustainable ecotourism should be promoted through not only the individual effort of a country but also through international cooperation.

Countries should develop national ecotourism strategies through a process of consultation in order to develop ecotourism in a sustainable manner.

Working group – C

PRODUCT DEVELOPMENT, MARKETING AND PROMOTION OF ECOTOURISM: Fostering sustainable products and consumers

Ecotourism will only bring benefits to conservation and communities if good quality, viable ecotourism products, which reflect market demand, are created and actively promoted. This working group was concerned with developing the right support structures, market knowledge, and attention to detail in product development, to enable this to happen.

The sixteen presentations at the working group covered:
- Government policies and priorities for ecotourism development – Indonesia, Germany and Venezuela.
- The management and development of ecotourism in protected areas – Quebec (Canada), Sao Paulo (Brazil), Italy, University of Valencia (Spain), and UNESCO.
- The position of intergovernmental, non-governmental and media organizations in ecotourism development and marketing, and its relationship with communities and conservation – International Labour Organisation, Conservation International, Retour Foundation, National Geographic Society -.
- Ecotourism initiatives by the private sector and partnership organisations – Earth Rhythms (Canada), Native Tourism Alliance (USA), PICE (Mexico), Casa Matsiguenka (Peru).

1. ISSUES DISCUSSED

The working group concentrated its debates on creating the right context for ecotourism development as well as on practical development and marketing issues. Throughout, there was concern that the nature of products developed and the messages put across to visitors should reflect the need to bring economic, environmental and social benefits.

The report on the preparatory conferences identified a number of challenges for ecotourism product development and marketing. These were:

- The failure of too many products, through lack of profitability, often due to poor feasibility assessment and business planning.
- Difficulties faced by small enterprises and community-based products in reaching markets cost effectively.
- Inconsistency in the quality of the visitor experience and in environmental management of ecotourism products.
- The need and opportunity to gain more benefit from visitors to support conservation and local communities, for example through stimulating more spending per head and reducing leakages from the local area.
- A continuing lack of public awareness of ecotourism issues, with few people specifically seeking out sustainable ecotourism products.

Participants in the working group were reminded of these challenges, which provided a context for the debates that followed.

In the light of these challenges, the report on the preparatory conferences identified five priorities:

- Creating the right structures for local communities, tourism enterprises, public bodies and NGOs to work together;
- Relating supply to demand, with a better knowledge of markets and how to reach them.
- Paying attention to all aspects of product quality, including design and management for sustainability as well as visitor satisfaction.
- Providing relevant support for communities and enterprises, which is locally delivered and tailored to the needs of communities and small enterprises.
- Strengthening the promotion of ecotourism messages and products, including promoting the concept of ecotourism as well as specific products.

This report takes each of these priority areas in turn and sets out the points and recommendations relating to them that emerged during the working group session.

2. KEY POINTS AND RECOMMENDATIONS

Structures and relationships for product development and marketing

Main recommendations resulting from the preparatory conferences:

- Address local community needs and opportunities.
- Recognise the key role of private sector businesses and strengthen their links with local communities.
- Strengthen networking between small enterprises and projects, so assisting market outreach and promoting common standards.
- Recognise protected areas as focal points for ecotourism products and marketing.
- Increase support from national and local government.

Key points arising from the Summit:

Recognising traditional values

Presentations at the working group emphasised that the principles of ecotourism are often enshrined in traditional values. Such values can influence the approach at a national level. For example, in Indonesia the national tourism policy is based on the principle of the 'Balance of Life' between exploitation and preservation of resources.

At a local level, many indigenous communities have values that are based on the stewardship of the earth's resources and hospitality towards visitors. These values must be respected. They provide a positive reason for assisting local communities to take their own decisions about the development and promotion of ecotourism and the way in which their natural resources and cultures are interpreted to visitors.

Building partnerships

The importance of establishing multi-stakeholder partnerships was underlined by many presentations and interventions. These can take various forms.

One way of assisting indigenous people to gain benefit from ecotourism is by helping them to form partnerships with organisations which can support and fund community projects, individual enterprises and joint ventures. An example is the North American Native Tourism Alliance.

Partnerships for ecotourism should be established between states, where appropriate. An example is the cooperation between Saharan states in a UNESCO pilot project, which is promoting cooperation in training, support for micro enterprises, and the identification and protection of natural and cultural resources.

More consideration should be given to involving tour operators, alongside communities and NGOs, in partnerships for successful ecotourism. An example is the project for the Development of Cultural and Ecotourism in the Mountainous Regions of Central Asia and the Himalayas. This even extends the partnership to tourists themselves – in one initiative, trekkers end their visit working with local people on social and conservation projects.

Linking conservation of biodiversity with direct economic benefits to local people

The role of ecotourism as a stimulus for the conservation of nature was strongly emphasised at the working group. This role is best played through providing a source of livelihood for local people which encourages and empowers them to preserve the biodiversity of their local area. The presentation by Conservation International (C.I.) confirmed the importance they place on ecotourism in their people-centred conservation approach, especially in the world's biodiversity hotspots, which contain millions of people living in poverty.

When challenged in debate about the effectiveness of ecotourism, C.I. cited numerous examples where it was generating significant conservation benefits. However, this requires ecotourism products to be based on integrated, participatory processes which take time to deliver results.

Strengthening the role of protected areas in ecotourism development

There was a specific recommendation that the key role of protected areas in the management and development of ecotourism should be recognised. In some cases they may require more resources to fulfil this role, although ecotourism may also provide a source of revenue.

It was recognised that protected area authorities need to work with local stakeholders on the development of ecotourism, and that appropriate structures should be established for this. Examples of parks working with local communities were provided by the approach of Parcs Québec in extending their network, and by the long-standing UNESCO Man and Biosphere model of evolving and adaptive management. In Italy, a national partnership for ecotourism has been established between the Federation of Parks, NGOs and private sector representatives.

A note of caution was sounded about the level of ecotourism activity to encourage actually within protected areas, rather than in surrounding locations, which may be more robust. There is a need for careful planning which reflects the resources and sensitivity of different areas and the type of designation. Further training and materials to improve the skills of protected area managers in ecotourism is required; an example presented at the workshop was the Toolkit for Sustainable Tourism in Wetlands.

Seeking a greater role for provincial and local authorities

There was a specific recommendation that provincial and local authorities should play a far more active role in ecotourism planning and support, providing a bridge between national policies and local communities. Such authorities often have responsibility for a range of services which affect ecotourism and also provide a long-lasting structure for developing, managing and supporting initiatives. However, more guidance should be given to local authorities on how to fulfil their role in ecotourism.

Understanding markets

Main recommendations from the preparatory conferences:
• Use more market research.
• Take a broad view of the market, recognising different segments.
• Study current visitor flows and local market conditions before product development takes place.

Key points arising from the Summit:

Understanding visitor motivations and disseminating research results

A number of interventions pointed to the need for more market research to provide data on existing and potential visitor profiles and motivations for visiting natural areas. This research should not only take place within source markets. It is important to understand more about the kinds of people who are already responding to ecotourism products within destinations.

It was recognised that part of the answer is to ensure the better use of existing market research. There was a specific recommendation that the results of the WTO studies of seven source markets should be made accessible, to the extent possible and/or through the corresponding national tourism administrations, to small ecotourism projects and firms in less developed countries.

Recognising ecotourism as more than a niche market

It was pointed out at the working group session that ecotourism should not be equated only with a niche market but also with a set of principles, especially concerning benefits to conservation and local communities. There was general agreement that too narrow a view should not be taken in identifying the potential market for ecotourism. In a paper entitled 'Moving Ecotourism beyond its niche' the National Geographical Society presented research that suggested that a sizeable market in the USA would respond to concepts of supporting conservation and the well-being of local people in their travel choice.

A number of the case studies presented at the working group session were catering for a domestic as well as an international market, and not only for people with a specialist interest in nature. It was suggested that it is important not to isolate ecotourism from the mainstream of tourism. Examples were given of day visitors from coastal resorts coming to inland cultural or natural heritage sites. These may provide serious management challenges in some cases, but also a valuable source of income for ecotourism initiatives.

The presentations and debate pointed to the need for more, well informed, market segmentation, enabling products and promotional strategies to be adapted to different requirements.

Avoiding false expectations

There was a call for better market assessment and business planning for individual projects, taking account of location, resource constraints, current visitor flows and performance of comparable products. This should help to avoid false expectations and the development of ecotourism in areas where it is unlikely to be successful.

Key components of ecotourism products

Main recommendations from the preparatory conferences:
- Address quality, authenticity and security.
- Give top priority to effective interpretation of nature and culture.
- Design and manage service facilities, such as accommodation and catering, to maximise sustainability.
- Address destination issues, such as infrastructure and transport, as well as individual product issues.
- Relate ecotourism to sustainable activity tourism, where appropriate.

Key points arising from the Summit:

Underlining the importance of authenticity and creative interpretation

The need for authenticity in ecotourism projects was strongly endorsed. The advantages of creative interpretation and the use of local guides were emphasised. An imaginative example of participatory interpretation was provided by the Earth Rhythms project in Manitoba, Canada, which is all about enabling visitors to "Live the story with real people".

During the plenary discussion, attention was drawn to the value of involving environmentalists, anthropologists and other specialists to ensure the accuracy of interpretation and to add depth to it, while accepting the importance of effective, accessible presentation involving local people.

Facilitating design and management for sustainability

A fundamental point made at the Summit is that ecotourism projects should embrace all aspects of sustainability, in the way they are developed and operated. Ecotourism should give a lead towards more sustainable tourism generally.

A number of examples of excellent environmentally sensitive design, in terms of both aesthetics and technical factors, were presented at the workshop. It was apparent that a wealth of knowledge is available internationally on this subject. The recent publication on ecolodges by The International Ecotourism Society provides an example. It is recommended that priority should be given to disseminating good practice in this field.

Some concern was expressed about the cost of low impact construction but it was stressed that this need not be more expensive than traditional techniques and can bring significant savings in operational costs. It is recommended that evidence about this is put across clearly.

The importance of personal security is recognised. It was pointed out that tour operators promoting ecotourism often face high costs in meeting obligations in this respect, which have to be taken into account.

Addressing the issue of access to ecotourism destinations and experiences

A number of interventions suggested that the issue of access is too often ignored in ecotourism planning and development. Three aspects of this were raised.

First, in some locations there is a need to facilitate access, where communities may be isolated. It was recommended that there is a need to work more closely with transport operators in ecotourism development.

Secondly, there is considerable concern that ecotourism policies and products should promote the use of environmentally friendly transport options, both to and within the destination. In Germany, for example, the promotion of cycling and walking is of fundamental importance in policies towards sustainable tourism and ecotourism.

Thirdly, there is a need to avoid discrimination against people with disabilities or other disadvantages in terms of access to ecotourism experiences.

Technical support for communities and enterprises

Main recommendations from the preparatory conferences:
- Provide relevant local training, devised with local people and enterprises to encourage participation.
- Encourage people to look together at the local resource and at ecotourism projects elsewhere.
- Provide well-targeted, accessible financial assistance.

Key points arising from the Summit:

Giving priority to capacity building

Many presentations emphasised the importance of capacity building within local communities. For example, human resource development was seen as a priority requirement in Indonesia and Venezuela. It was emphasised that capacity building requires time and commitment. There was also a call for more financial assistance for training.

A particular point was made that, as well as supporting businesses, capacity building and specific training programmes in the field of ecotourism could be directed at young people at the start of their working life. An example of this was provided by the Sao Paulo Green Belt Biosphere Reserve and their establishment of eco-job training centres.

46

Helping ecotourism projects to learn from each other

It was agreed that a lot could be achieved by exchanging experiences between different projects. The value of the suggestion, arising from the preparatory conferences, of promoting twinning and multi-lateral links between projects, was illustrated in the presentations.

Raising the profile and knowledge of tourism within donor agencies, and the quality of applications to them

It was felt that donor agencies should take tourism more seriously. Many have no specific strategy for supporting tourism or particular skills or knowledge about ecotourism. This should be rectified.

However, the responsibility of applicants in seeking funding was also recognised. It was pointed out that projects seeking funding must have a well-prepared business plan.

Some delegates commented that there was not enough knowledge about the various sources of financial assistance, including international donor agencies, bilateral support programmes, and assistance available from NGOs. There was a specific recommendation that a database of information on this should be created and disseminated.

Structuring financial and technical assistance to the requirements of small businesses and local communities

There was considerable debate about appropriate forms of support for ecotourism projects.

A presentation at the workshop on the International Labour Organization's sustainable tourism project with indigenous communities in Bolivia, Ecuador and Peru set out a structured approach, with programmes of assistance at a micro level (for community-based enterprises), at a medium level (for clusters of tourism initiatives within community networks, and for local government), and at a macro level (to strengthen organisations, certification and marketing within states).

A clear message from delegates was that assistance should be in a form that can be accessed by small and micro businesses and local communities and one that is relevant to their needs. Specific recommendations were that:

- donor agencies should provide more schemes which channel assistance directly to enterprises and communities rather than through national governments;
- funding should be available in small packets, with a low minimum level, relevant to the size of small enterprises;
- there is a need for micro-credit schemes.

There was a call for the application of fiscal incentives as a tool to encourage tourism service providers to develop and manage their enterprises more sustainably.

A further specific recommendation was for the establishment of a network of ecotourism advisors or mentors as a readily available source of help for small ecotourism businesses.

Promoting ecotourism messages and products

Main recommendations from the preparatory conferences:
- Promote ecotourism as a concept, with an international awareness campaign.
- Grasp the significant opportunity presented by the Internet.
- Use a range of marketing techniques and partners.
- Provide comprehensive and educative information at all stages, before, during and after the visit.
- Create loyal ambassadors among tourists.

Key points arising from the Summit:

Raising public awareness of tourism impacts, ecotourism principles and actions to take

During the working group session, a number of comments were made on the importance to promote the actual concept of ecotourism, its ideals and values, rather than simply ecotourism products. However, there was a little concern that the word 'ecotourism' may actually be putting some people off. It was agreed that principles and goals are what is important; people should not get hung up on terminology.

The report on the preparatory conferences suggested that there should be a coordinated international campaign to promote ecotourism principles and concepts, but that this might not simply be a generic campaign; rather it should promote specific action that visitors could take. As an example of this, it was recommended that the process of visitors and tour operators making financial donations to local community projects or conservation causes should be more actively promoted, with a vision of this becoming the norm rather than the exception.

A strong recommendation was made in the presentation by the Retour Foundation, an NGO working with indigenous communities, that tourists should be provided with detailed information about the effect of their travelling.

Promoting mutual understanding of cultural differences and sensitivities

It was recommended that information for visitors should include how to respect the local culture of their hosts and the sensitivity of the local environment. At the same time, there was a recommendation that indigenous and local communities should be provided with information about the culture and expectations of their visitors.

Working effectively with tour operators and the media

The importance of tour operators was referred to on several occasions. There was a specific recommendation that priority should be given to involving and educating local incoming tour operators and agents within destinations. On the other hand, some delegates recommended that ecotourism principles should be promoted more heavily amongst international tour operators, including the larger companies.

The strong influence of media reports and travel guides, which can be both damaging and highly beneficial to ecotourism, was emphasised during the plenary session. It was recommended that travel writers should be introduced to genuine, interesting stories about real people and experiences, rather than bland details of product.

Using the Internet as a communication medium at all points in the tourism chain

There was widespread agreement about the importance of the Internet for promoting ecotourism products. One comment highlighted its value amongst the large market of independent travellers, where it can be used for exchange of information and testimonials amongst visitors and for providing information within destinations as well as prior to departure. A high priority should be given to helping small enterprises and community initiatives link to appropriate technology.

Raising confidence through branded products

Branding of ecotourism products was considered to offer more opportunities. An example was a proposal to establish a world-wide brand of ecolodges with strong conservation credentials.

Gaining support for ecotourism amongst future visitors

Discussion at the workshop echoed the need, expressed in the preparatory conferences, to promote the concept of ecotourism to children and young people, as a receptive audience and as the travellers of the future.

Finally, the results from many successful projects presented during the Summit reaffirmed the importance of delivering a quality experience, leading to word of mouth recommendation, as the best form of marketing. This will increase the volume of tourists who are committed to ecotourism principles, who become ambassadors for conservation, and who have a greater understanding of different cultures around the world.

Working group – D

MONITORING COSTS AND BENEFITS OF ECOTOURISM: Ensuring equitable distribution among all stakeholders

In many ecotourism strategies the aim is to reduce the costs of ecotourism and ensuring that a whole range of benefits are obtained for local communities, the environment, visitors and other stakeholders. However, unless there is a system for monitoring the impacts of ecotourism, then the success of new strategies and actions will not be known. This working group was concerned with effective processes for checking on impacts and improving the distribution of benefits.

Eighteen presentations were made to the working group, covering:

- The relationship between indigenous people and ecotourism – Quebec, Equations (India), U.S.A.
- Poverty and managing equitable distribution – South Africa, Sri Lanka, Ghana
- International guidelines for monitoring costs and benefits – UNCTAD, IBST (International Bureau of Social tourism), Australia, Canada
- World heritage protection – UNESCO, Indonesia, Uganda
- Monitoring small and medium enterprises – Ethiopia, Madagascar
- Public sector role – Balearics (Spain)
- Specific methodologies and national examples – Kenya, Brazil, Yugoslavia
- Social aspects and better access to ecotourism – IBST, Equations (India)

1. ISSUES DISCUSSED

The following points were debated during the working group session.

- New ecotourism cost/benefit evaluation methods that would highlight the social and economic benefits for local populations, as well as the limitations of the financial benefits generated compared to other forms of tourism, notably mass tourism.
- Appropriate legal and institutional mechanisms to facilitate and make effective the systematic participation of local communities in the overall ecotourism process, including policy definition, planning, management and monitoring.
- Financial and fiscal mechanisms to ensure that a significant proportion of the income generated from ecotourism remains with the local community or serves conservation purposes.
- Methods to ensure the permanent control of impacts through the adaptation of carrying capacity methodologies to ecotourism development, including the definition of damage warning indicators and disturbance gauges for protected sites and other natural areas.
- Distribution mechanisms to share the benefits of ecotourism development in order to reinvest a proportion of the revenues generated in protected areas.
- Methods to assist understanding and measurement of social costs, benefits and change (i.e. changes in the behaviour and habits of the local population) so as to limit the negative consequences, to maximise social benefits for host communities and to improve attitudes, awareness and respect towards the protection of the environment.
- Specific management and monitoring procedures for different types of ecotourism sites, (i.e. desert zones and islands), concerning such aspects as water and waste management, the management of scarce resources, and others.
- Evaluation of appropriate price levels to ensure sufficient returns for firms, suitable redistribution in favour of local populations and that correspond to the purchasing power of tourism demand.

- Ensuring that the principles of "polluter pays" and "user pays" will ensure genuine protection of the environment whilst guaranteeing ecotourism development.

The working group endeavoured to bring together development strategies aimed at differentiating ecotourism from traditional tourism and creating a real balance to achieve the desired equitable distribution between all the stakeholders.

As a result of the presentations and the debates during the working group session, guidelines and directions towards concrete solutions were devised. These solutions challenge traditional tourism development policies that, as was emphasised by the contributors, must not merely consider ecotourism as a priority but as a tourism development catalyst, thus providing a new approach to tourism development as a whole. This was particularly highlighted in the contributions by the delegates from Kenya, Brazil, India and Serbia.

2. KEY POINTS AND RECOMMENDATIONS

For this catalytic role of ecotourism to really be effective, it is necessary to consider recommendations relating to the main pillars of this topic, namely monitoring costs, monitoring benefits, and equitable distribution. Some global recommendations also emerged from the working group.

Monitoring costs of ecotourism

Main recommendations from the preparatory conferences:
- Determine the economic costs of providing suitable infrastructure, including energy and transport, resources such as water, and waste treatment.
- Use indicators such as site stress to monitor environmental costs.
- Consider factors such as the disturbance of traditional lifestyles in determining social costs.
- Take an integrated approach to determining costs, such as effect on employment in other sectors, such as agriculture.
- Research specific management and monitoring procedures for different types of ecotourism sites, e.g. deserts and islands.
- Research methods to ensure the permanent control of impacts, including damage warning indicators for protected sites and other natural areas.

Key points arising from the Summit:

The presentations showed that for ecoutourism to develop sustainably it needs direct as well as indirect support from the public sector at the national and local levels.

Recognising costs relating to environmental management

The conflict between protecting nature and ecotourism development induces extra costs which ecotourism operators must bear. In the case of Sri Lanka for example, with respect to wildlife, the problems associated with the protection of the elephants must be managed in such a way that the local population could also be able to live in total security, particularly the farmers. In this particular case specific planning guidelines must be drawn up, which include protection barriers, requiring very heavy investment. This need for large financial resources impedes the development of ecotourism and can rupture the sustainable development process in these destinations.

This situation can be particularly serious in mass tourism destinations as illustrated by the presentation on the Balearic Islands in which it was argued that there is a direct relationship between high tourist numbers and the attractiveness of the destination. In this case, there is a conflict between tourism development and economic development because of the extra costs on the environment, resulting in the deterioration of the tourism situation in these destinations.

Taking all development and operational costs into account, including training

Ecotourism itself engenders extra costs, notably in terms of funding training. This important point was much discussed during the sessions. Indeed, ecotourism often implies heavier equipment expenditure and more skilled personnel than are required in traditional tourism. Therefore, preliminary training funding programmes must be introduced, and this can harm the competitiveness of the ecotourism product in a very competitive market. As a result, the profitability of ecotourism projects may be deemed insufficient. Examples from France for instance show that quite often the financing of training must come from public funds, which implies that in certain developing countries, the financing of ecotourism training must be included in international cooperation programmes.

Considering the full costs of transition to ecotourism

The cost of protecting nature generally implies very high expenditure and can be the cause of usage conflict in economic terms but also in social terms. This is the case in India for example where, in some highly populated regions, ecotourism development replaces certain agricultural production activities that must be abandoned to safeguard the endowments of protected areas. In such cases, the creation of jobs for tour guides and wardens does not compensate for the jobs lost in the agricultural sector, and this can cause tension between the local population and ecotourism operators when the cost of reconversion of agricultural populations are not taken into account in public policies.

Monitoring benefits of ecotourism

Main recommendations from the preparatory conferences:
- Take account of local income benefits and tax receipts.
- Consider improvement in local employment, living conditions and social services.
- Measure the local population's satisfaction through surveys.
- Use tourism satellite accounting to show impacts on different sectors.
- Develop new evaluation methods to take account of wider benefits and costs

Key points arising from the Summit:

The discussions during the working group session showed that the benefits of ecotourism are not as obvious as might be first thought. These benefits can be the cause of problems and sometimes controversy.

Being realistic about financial benefits

The financial benefits, in terms of fiscal and parafiscal receipts, must be considered as particularly important for local populations. However, the examples presented during the sessions show that these benefits only become significant after many years. Case studies from Madagascar demonstrate that in the short term fiscal and parafiscal receipts generated by ecotourism activity are weak and cannot finance the environmental protection that is necessary for high quality tourism products. Furthermore, these examples show that these benefits are very difficult to distribute amongst public and private stakeholders.

Using ecotourism benefits to alleviate poverty

The benefits of ecotourism should be orientated principally towards the poorest local populations. This is the objective of the many programmes presented during the Summit such as those in South Africa, Ghana and Uganda. From this point of view, ecotourism is better adapted than traditional commercial tourism to achieve this objective. However, as the presentation from India emphasised, ecotourism is a type of tourism development that can harm the traditional activities of the poorer populations (i.e. agriculture). This means that the benefits of ecotourism are not always sufficient to provide a significant contribution to the problems of extreme poverty and even in certain cases it can harm the very means of subsistence of very poor rural populations. Therefore, the assertion that developing ecotourism is a good method of solving the problems of poverty in developing countries should be expressed with caution, spelling out the conditions for this to occur.

Emphasising the merits of ecotourism in benefiting small enterprises

The benefits in terms of liberalisation of international exchanges in the GATS agreement framework should facilitate access to tourism development for all countries including LCDs (Least Developed Countries). However, as the speaker from UNCTAD pointed out during the debates and during the presentations at the Summit, traditional tourism tends to mostly benefit large enterprises. This is not the case of ecotourism, which should therefore be favoured in commercial international negotiations. Furthermore, this was emphasised during the session on international cooperation, which clearly demonstrated that tourism was a privileged element of regional cooperation benefiting primarily small and medium size enterprises.

Taking full account of associated benefits

The presentations and debates showed that the balance between costs and benefits are not always obvious to justify ecotourism development in economic and social development polices. However, several new points were brought to the debates proving that the benefits of ecotourism are much more numerous and important if some major elements which are often forgotten or ignored are considered.

In particular, two very positive points concerning ecotourism were discussed after the presentations by the IBST (International Bureau of Social Tourism):
- On the one hand, ecotourism benefits tourists by giving them the choice to enjoy a different type of tourism than traditional tourism. However, this benefit is only fully accountable if it is available to the whole population such as the young, the elderly and insofar as it is possible for the handicapped.
- On the other hand, ecotourism favours the initiatives of non-profit organisations and cooperatives, which generally have important direct and indirect impacts, benefiting local and indigenous communities.

The equitable distribution of benefits amongst stakeholders

Main recommendations from the preparatory conferences:
- Establish financial and fiscal mechanisms to ensure that a significant proportion of income generated from ecotourism remains in the local community or serves conservation.
- Put in place distribution mechanisms which reinvest a proportion of the revenues generated in the protected areas.
- Consider the impact of price levels on the distribution of benefits.

Key points arising from the Summit:

It emerged from the presentations and debates that the principles of ecotourism are more of an aspiration than a reality for many countries, regions and local and indigenous populations, despite significant progress.

Equitable distribution is an aspiration for many stakeholders because there exist today a multitude of initiatives and ecotourism product development projects everywhere in the world. Nevertheless, a survey carried out in Australia showed that there are thousands of ecotourism schemes, which would suggest that the economic weight of ecotourism in world tourism is becoming increasingly important and could support the efforts to achieve a better distribution between all stakeholders of the benefits of tourism development.

The equitable distribution between all stakeholders is strengthened because of the prevalence of small and medium sized enterprises in the development of ecotourism. The example provided by Ethiopia, discussing the role of SMEs in the development of ecotourism, shows that the benefits of ecotourism can be turned from aspiration into reality if tourism development associated with ecotourism is sufficiently important.

The equitable distribution between all stakeholders will only become a significant reality when the benefits to be distributed are great enough. However, the contributions from the representatives of the poorest regions and countries emphasised that this is not the case everywhere in the world. One of the reasons put forward by UNCTAD is the lack of comparative studies to provide useful information on the successes and failures of different methods of equitable distribution amongst stakeholders. The aim would be to establish demonstration projects which would serve as references to ensure that the development of ecotourism will also provide real equitable distribution between all stakeholders.

Global recommendations

Main recommendations from the preparatory conferences:
- Ensure a constant monitoring of ecotourism activities to ensure they are meeting the required objectives.
- Determine distinct quantitative evaluation criteria or a range of standards, in cooperation with national and local authorities.
- Establish an evolutionary management system, including monitoring, based on public-private partnership.

Key points arising from the Summit:

The following overall conclusions were drawn from the presentations and the debates in the working group and were presented during the plenary session:
- The existing ecotourism cost, benefit and impact evaluation methods, should be reviewed and new methods should be devised which would highlight the social and economic benefits for local populations and compare these with the costs, benefits and impacts of other forms of tourism and other economic alternatives.
- Appropriate legal, political, institutional and funding mechanisms should be established in order to facilitate and make effective the participation of local communities in the overall ecotourism process, including definition, planning, management, monitoring and conflict resolution.
- Indigenous communities and groups should be involved from the very beginning in the decision process about ecotourism including the assessment and monitoring of costs, benefits and impacts in particular with respect to their culture and traditions.
- Financial and fiscal mechanisms should be implemented to ensure that a significant proportion of the income generated from ecotourism remains with the local community and is reinvested for environmental and cultural conservation purposes.
- A permanent and consistent monitoring of ecotourism impacts should be implemented as an integral part of the overall management for protected sites and other natural areas, and therefore the existing approaches such as carrying capacity methodologies, damage warning indicators and other monitoring instruments should be adapted.

In addition, the participants in the working group proposed a recommendation to the plenary session of the World Ecotourism Summit to affirm the clear and inalienable rights of indigenous communities, in terms of international legal instruments, to self-determination and prior informed consent in ecotourism development.

4. REPORTS FROM THE SPECIAL FORUMS

On the final day of the Summit, two special forums were held in order to discuss the perspective of ecotourism businesses (Forum 1) and the issue of development cooperation (Forum 2). The results of these forums are presented in the pages which follow.

In addition, a **Ministerial Forum** was held. This forum enabled a wide range of countries to describe their policies and activities in the field of ecotourism. The majority of speakers were Ministers of Tourism or senior officials from the ministry of tourism in the respective countries, but some countries were represented by their environment ministry or their diplomatic representative in Canada.

The countries making interventions at the Ministerial Forum included

Andorra	Malawi
Algeria	Nigeria
Bangladesh	Pakistan
Cambodia	Paraguay
Cuba	Philippines
Cyprus	Romania
Ecuador	Sri Lanka
Egypt	Uruguay
India	

Each country representative explained the state of development of ecotourism in their country and the problems and challenges being faced. All of them reiterated their commitment to sustainability principles in tourism and set out the steps being taken to develop and promote ecotourism.

FORUM 1: THE ECOTOURISM BUSINESS PERSPECTIVE

This forum concerned the practical experiences and needs of private sector businesses operating in ecotourism. It centred on four presentations from enterprises based in the US Virgin Islands, Canada, Panama and India. There was also a considerable period for discussion with many points raised from the floor.

1 ISSSUES DISCUSSED

The need for government support for small ecotourism operators

Ecotourism operators often find themselves at a disadvantage because of specific government regulations. For example, in destination countries where business visas have a limited time before expiry, this may result in on-ground tour leaders or facilitators having to leave the country prematurely.

Other problems result from a lack of government action. One example is the lack of assistance for operators to develop new tours in destinations. This is a big problem for operators, since research and testing potential products on the ground may take some years, but once products are developed, other companies may replicate this new package, with no research costs. Developing new packages is becoming increasingly difficult.

Some problems occur when the ethics of the destination government are in conflict with the principles of ecotourism. Some ethically minded operators pull out of the destination, which ironically leaves the field (and their repeat clients and developmental groundwork) available to less ethically-oriented tour operators.

Problems of financing ecotourism operations

It was generally agreed that obtaining finance to initiate ecotourism operations is extremely difficult; it is often non-existent. Many operations are only possible by using personal savings or obtaining personal loans. The conventional banking sector is not currently helpful until after success is achieved, when assistance is least necessary.

Other costs concerns are related to proposed certification programs, which operators fear they will not be able to buy into; additionally, they do not have the time to engage in the often lengthy and difficult certification procedure.

Cost and lack of support for research and development

Operators agreed that it is difficult and expensive to research and develop new ecotourism packages in many destinations. Also, that when established, there are no mechanisms to prevent other operators from copying their packages.

Lack of integrated objectives

Some ecotourism operators started with worthy but limited motivations, such as a strong desire for environmental conservation or protection of endangered places or species. However, they discover that unless local jobs are created and operational profitability is an objective, the business will have difficulties or will fail, thus also failing to achieve the original objective. It was felt that entrepreneurs need to internalise the principles of sustainability in their business, and that if they emphasise only one or two perspectives, they will not achieve sustainability over the long term. Those businesses focusing on economic perspectives also need to integrate community and environmental perspectives; reciprocally, those businesses focusing on community benefits also need to consider environmental issues relating both to the community and their business. In this way, there is a greater likelihood that the business will be sustainable over the long term, whereas if other perspectives are not considered, long-term business viability is unlikely.

Environmental destruction

Operators expressed that poaching is an issue in a number of destinations, as well as slash-and-burn agriculture and other practices, which destroy forests and other habitats. These unsustainable land use practices are greatly affecting the quality of some destinations. Operators could improve environmental conditions at destinations by involving more local communities, bringing economic alternatives, and by this way providing incentives to preserve the environment; however, without government support it is difficult for them to tackle these problems alone.

2. CONCLUSIONS AND RECOMMENDATIONS

Separate policies are required for ecotourism, distinguishing it from mainstream tourism operations

Mechanisms should be developed to facilitate start-up funding for small tourism operations.

Governments or other agencies at the destinations should examine ways to provide assistance to ecotourism operations researching and introducing new packages. As an example, the Malaysia Tourism Commission has cost-shared advertising of new packages for a certain time period, which benefited both the operator and the destination.

It was recommended that NGOs should play a stronger role in providing up to date research information (destinations or markets) to operators.

Involve those who are part of a problem in the solution

It is recommended that all stakeholders should be involved in solving ecotourism-related problems, especially those who are part of a problem. For example, in India, there has been recent interaction between poachers, NGOs, forest officials, and the ecotourism facilitator.

Take an integrated approach

Ecotourism operators should take an integrated operational perspective from the outset. This will involve: protecting the environment that visitors wish to experience; providing local jobs so that the environment is not endangered by unsustainable local use (e.g., slash and burn agriculture); providing desired visitor interactions with local people; and focusing on business profitability to sustain the other objectives.

It was suggested that creative businesses can create profit streams within their operations through applying sustainability principles. For example, in Maho Bay Camps (US Virgin Islands), sustainable technologies contribute to cost savings as well as to guest satisfaction. Waste aluminium, glass and plastic is used in craft workshops and converted into products for sale, thus employing locals, providing guest entertainment, generating revenues, and removing waste from the island.

It is recommended that public-private partnerships be encouraged as a method of assisting business start-ups, as well as meeting joint objectives, involving business, government, NGOs, or development agencies.

Provide adequate remuneration to local employees at destinations

It was recommended that local people be paid significant wages by operators. This helps ensure ongoing reliability and quality performance, and acts as a model for others. For example, in India, slash and burn agriculture is reducing, unused cargo boats are being converted to viable house-boat operations, and poachers are being transformed into respected, well-paid employees.

The portion of total consumer package costs which destinations receive should be critically examined, since at present the average percentage is relatively low.

FORUM 2:
DEVELOPMENT COOPERATION FOR ECOTOURISM

The development cooperation forum concentrated on the role of development agencies in providing financial and technical support for ecotourism.

Most of the speakers were representing international or bilaterial donor agencies or consultancies, including: GEF/UNDP Small Grants Programme, SNV Netherlands, Swiss Association for International Cooperation, German Technical Cooperation Agency (GTZ), and the Inter-American Development Bank, besides the World Tourism Organization. The Minister of Tourism from Angola provided a recipient country perspective.

1. ISSUES DISCUSSED

The need for international cooperation

The WTO and government representatives emphasised the crucial role of international cooperation in promoting a sustainable development of ecotourism, particularly in less developed countries.

The WTO, as the UNDP's executing agency for tourism development, is a catalyst for generating finance and can organise international cooperation. With its technical expertise WTO can provide guidelines and solutions to achieve an appropriate balance between the economic development of tourism and sustainability. Thus WTO can facilitate the development of new types of international cooperation, motivating other agencies towards a common objective with public/private sector partnerships.

This need for regional cooperation on ecotourism projects, particularly in Africa, was pointed out by Angola's Minister of Tourism. An example of this kind of support was given through the RETOSA / SADEC tourism projects.

Speakers looked in turn at issues relating to bilateral, regional and international cooperation.

New objectives for international cooperation

There has been a notable change in the way development agencies are treating tourism projects. Whereas previously there was an emphasis on the quantity of tourism development and revenue generated, there is now greater concern for the quality of the end result and a range of social and environmental as well as purely economic objectives. The revision of tourism master plans has reflected this change of emphasis. This has led to a focus on the capacity of local communities to engage in, and benefit from, tourism.

A growing number of players

In the past development cooperation was mainly provided by a small number of international organisations dealing with states at a government level. Now there are many more agencies providing relevant assistance, including NGOs, regional organisations, bilateral aid schemes and private sector bodies. Some of these new forms of cooperation are particularly appropriate for ecotourism as they are often focused on generating self-help in communities (e.g. the approach of SNV Netherlands).

New structures and levels for cooperation

International cooperation itself has changed. Cooperation is now located in an inter-regional context and its focus is on decentralised programmes. This regional cooperation is well adapted to ecotourism. A new priority is given to training and capacity building, as key issues to strengthen ecotourism, and to providing support for indigenous organisations.

2. CONCLUSIONS AND RECOMMENDATIONS

Provide more support for capacity building

The recognition of the need to support capacity building, mentioned above, is important. A further focus on this in all assistance programmes should be encouraged.

Ensure that projects assisted are viable

Too frequently in the past assistance has been provided for ecotourism projects which may not be viable in the long term, after assistance has come to a end. More attention should be given to feasibility assessment.

Make sure that local communities are involved and benefiting

Development agencies should pay attention to organisational and participatory structures in recipient destinations. It is very important that there is local participation in programmes supported. A number of comments made stressed the importance of organisational strengthening and the role of local authorities.

Raise the profile of ecotourism within development agencies

In general, development agencies are still paying too little attention to ecotourism. They should be encouraged to develop strategies for their work in this sector. This should apply to individual agencies and collectively, as there is a need for more coordination between agencies in their work in this area.

Provide a range of levels of financial support

In the past financial assistance has tended to be provided in large amounts, relevant to larger scale projects. There is now a need for a full range of types and levels of assistance, including programmes suitable for very small enterprises and community-based initiatives, and for medium sized projects which are locally owned, yet with significant costs as well as local impacts.

5. PREPARING AND ADOPTING THE FINAL DECLARATION

The Summit closed with a final plenary session which addressed the text of the Quebec Declaration on Ecotourism.

An initial draft of the declaration had been circulated to delegates at the start of the Summit. All delegates were invited to submit written comments on the text, including specific recommendations for amendments, improvements and additions. A total of 160 written comments were received by the deadline at the end of the second full day of the Summit. WTO and UNEP also received verbal representation from a number of individuals and groups, including representatives of indigenous communities and of NGOs working with such communities. All these comments were carefully assessed by WTO and UNEP and taken into consideration in the preparation of a second draft.

The second draft of the declaration was circulated to delegates at the start of the third day. This draft formed the basis of the debate during the final plenary session. Many delegates made further comments and recommendations on it from the floor. These interventions were recorded. All of them were assessed and used by WTO and UNEP to produce a final text of the declaration on the day following the Summit. This text was then made available to delegates and others on the Internet.

The text of the Quebec Declaration on Ecotourism is reproduced in full on the following pages.

6. THE QUÉBEC DECLARATION ON ECOTOURISM

In the framework of the UN International Year of Ecotourism, 2002, under the aegis of the United Nations Environment Programme (UNEP) and the World Tourism Organization (WTO), over one thousand participants coming from 132 countries, from the public, private and non-governmental sectors met at the World Ecotourism Summit, hosted in Québec City, Canada, by Tourisme Québec and the Canadian Tourism Commission, between 19 and 22 May 2002.

The Québec Summit represented the culmination of 18 preparatory meetings held in 2001 and 2002, involving over 3,000 representatives from national and local governments including the tourism, environment and other administrations, private ecotourism businesses and their trade associations, non-governmental organizations, academic institutions and consultants, intergovernmental organizations, and indigenous and local communities.

This document takes into account the preparatory process, as well as the discussions held during the Summit. It is the result of a multistakeholder dialogue, although it is not a negotiated document. Its main purpose is the setting of a preliminary agenda and a set of recommendations for the development of ecotourism activities in the context of sustainable development.

The participants at the Summit acknowledge the World Summit on Sustainable Development (WSSD) in Johannesburg, August/September 2002, as the ground-setting event for international policy in the next 10 years, and emphasize that, as a leading industry, the sustainability of tourism should be a priority at WSSD due to its potential contribution to poverty alleviation and environmental protection in endangered ecosystems. Participants therefore request the UN, its organizations and member governments represented at this Summit to disseminate the following Declaration and other results from the World Ecotourism Summit at the WSSD.

The participants to the World Ecotourism Summit, aware of the limitations of this consultative process to incorporate the input of the large variety of ecotourism stakeholders, particularly non-governmental organizations (NGOs) and local and indigenous communities,

Recognize that ecotourism embraces the principles of sustainable tourism, concerning the economic, social and environmental impacts of tourism. It also embraces the following specific principles which distinguish it from the wider concept of sustainable tourism:

- Contributes actively to the conservation of natural and cultural heritage,
- Includes local and indigenous communities in its planning, development and operation, and contributing to their well-being,
- Interprets the natural and cultural heritage of the destination to visitors,
- Lends itself better to independent travellers, as well as to organized tours for small size groups.

Acknowledge that tourism has significant and complex social, economic and environmental implications, which can bring both benefits and costs to the environment and local communities,

Consider the growing interest of people in travelling to natural areas, both on land and sea,

Recognize that ecotourism has provided a leadership role in introducing sustainability practices to the tourism sector,

Emphasize that ecotourism should continue to contribute to make the overall tourism industry more sustainable, by increasing economic and social benefits for host communities, actively contributing to the conservation of natural resources and the cultural integrity of host communities, and by increasing awareness of all travellers towards the conservation of natural and cultural heritage,

Recognize the cultural diversity associated with many natural areas, particularly because of the historical presence of local and indigenous communities, of which some have maintained their traditional knowledge, uses and practices many of which have proven to be sustainable over the centuries,

Reiterate that funding for the conservation and management of biodiverse and culturally rich protected areas has been documented to be inadequate worldwide,

Recognize further that many of these areas are home to peoples often living in poverty, who frequently lack adequate health care, education facilities, communications systems, and other infrastructure required for genuine development opportunity,

Affirm that different forms of tourism, especially ecotourism, if managed in a sustainable manner can represent a valuable economic opportunity for local and indigenous populations and their cultures and for the conservation and sustainable use of nature for future generations and can be a leading source of revenues for protected areas,

Emphasize that at the same time, wherever and whenever tourism in natural and rural areas is not properly planned, developed and managed, it contributes to the deterioration of natural landscapes, threats to wildlife and biodiversity, marine and coastal pollution, poor water quality, poverty, displacement of indigenous and local communities, and the erosion of cultural traditions,

Acknowledge that ecotourism development must consider and respect the land and property rights, and, where recognized, the right to self-determination and cultural sovereignty of indigenous and local communities, including their protected, sensitive and sacred sites as well as their traditional knowledge,

Stress that to achieve equitable social, economic and environmental benefits from ecotourism and other forms of tourism in natural areas, and to minimize or avoid potential negative impacts, participative planning mechanisms are needed that allow local and indigenous communities, in a transparent way, to define and regulate the use of their areas at the local level, including the right to opt out of tourism development,

Understand that small and micro businesses seeking to meet social and environmental objectives are key partners in ecotourism and are often operating in a development climate that does not provide suitable financial and marketing support for ecotourism,

Recognize that to improve the chances of survival of small-, medium-, and micro enterprises further understanding of the ecotourism market will be required through market research, specialized credit instruments for tourism businesses, grants for external costs, incentives for the use of sustainable energy and innovative technical solutions, and an emphasis on developing skills not only in business but within government and those seeking to support business solutions,

Accept the need to avoid discrimination between people, whether by race, gender or other personal circumstances, with respect to their involvement in ecotourism as consumers or suppliers,

Recognize that visitors have a responsibility to the sustainability of the destination and the global environment through their travel choice, behaviour and activities, and that therefore it is important to communicate to them the qualities and sensitivities of destinations,

In light of the above, the participants to the World Ecotourism Summit, having met in Québec City, from 19 to 22 May 2002, produced a series of recommendations, which they propose to governments, the private sector, non-governmental organizations, community-based associations, academic and research institutions, inter-governmental organizations, international financial institutions, development assistance agencies, and indigenous and local communities, as follows:

A. To national, regional and local governments

1. *formulate* national, regional and local ecotourism policies and development strategies that are consistent with the overall objectives of sustainable development, and to do so through a wide consultation process with those who are likely to become involved in, affect, or be affected by ecotourism activities;

2. *guarantee* -in conjunction with local and indigenous communities, the private sector, NGOs and all ecotourism stakeholders- the protection of nature, local and indigenous cultures and specially traditional knowledge, genetic resources, rights to land and property, as well as rights to water;

3. *ensure* the involvement, appropriate participation and necessary coordination of all the relevant public institutions at the national, provincial and local level, (including the establishment of inter-ministerial working groups as appropriate) at different stages in the ecotourism process, while at the same time opening and

facilitating the participation of other stakeholders in   ecotourism-related decisions. Furthermore, adequate budgetary mechanisms and appropriate legislative frameworks need to *be set up* to allow implementation of the objectives and goals set up by these multistakeholder bodies;

4. *include* in the above framework the necessary regulatory and monitoring mechanisms at the national, regional and local levels, including objective sustainability indicators jointly agreed with all stakeholders and environmental impact assessment studies to be used as feedback mechanism.   Results of monitoring should be made available to the general public;

5. *develop* regulatory mechanisms for internalization of environmental costs in all aspects of the tourism product, including international transport;

6. *develop* the local and municipal capacity to implement growth management tools such as zoning, and participatory land-use planning not only in protected areas but in buffer zones and other ecotourism development zones;

7. *use* internationally approved and reviewed guidelines to develop certification schemes, ecolabels and other voluntary initiatives geared towards sustainability in ecotourism, encouraging private operators to join such schemes and promoting their recognition by consumers. However, certification systems should reflect regional and local criteria. Build capacity and provide financial support to make these schemes accessible to small and medium enterprises (SMEs). In addition, monitoring and a regulatory framework are necessary to support effective implementation of these schemes;

8. *ensure* the provision of technical, financial and human resources development support to micro, small and medium-sized firms, which are the core of ecotourism, with a view to enable them to start, grow and develop their businesses in a sustainable manner;

9. *define* appropriate policies, management plans, and interpretation programmes for visitors, and earmark adequate sources of funding for natural areas to manage visitor numbers, protect vulnerable ecosystems, and the sustainable use of sensitive habitats. Such plans should include clear norms, direct and indirect management strategies, and regulations with the funds to ensure monitoring of social and environmental impacts for all ecotourism businesses operating in the area, as well as for tourists wishing to visit them;

10. *include* micro, small and medium-sized ecotourism companies, as well as community-based and NGO-based ecotourism operations in the overall promotional strategies and programmes carried out by the National Tourism Administration, both in the international and domestic markets;

11. *encourage* and *support* the creation of regional networks and cooperation for promotion and marketing of ecotourism products at the international and national levels;

12. *provide* incentives to tourism operators and other service providers (such as marketing and promotion advantages) for them to adopt ecotourism principles and make their operations more environmentally, socially and culturally responsible;

13. *ensure* that basic environmental and health standards are identified and met by all ecotourism development even in the most rural areas. This should include aspects such as site selection, planning, design, the treatment of solid waste, sewage, and the protection of watersheds, etc., and *ensure* also that ecotourism development strategies are not undertaken by governments without investment in sustainable infrastructure and the reinforcement of local/municipal capabilities to regulate and monitor such aspects;

14. *institute* baseline environmental impact assessment (EIA) studies and surveys that record the social environmental state of destinations, with special attention to endangered species, and *invest,* or *support* institutions that invest in research programmes on ecotourism and sustainable tourism;

15. *support* the further implementation of the international principles, guidelines and codes of ethics for sustainable tourism (e.g. such as those proposed by UNEP, WTO, the Convention on Biological Diversity, the UN Commission on Sustainable Development and the International Labor Organization) for the enhancement of international and national legal frameworks, policies and master plans to implement the concept of sustainable development into tourism;

16. *consider* as one option the reallocation of tenure and management of public lands, from extractive or intensive productive sectors to tourism combined with conservation, wherever this is likely to improve the net social, economic and environmental benefit for the community concerned;

17. *promote* and *develop* educational programmes addressed to children and young people to enhance awareness about nature conservation and sustainable use, local and indigenous cultures and their relationship with ecotourism;

18. *promote* collaboration between outbound tour operators and incoming operators and other service providers and NGOs at the destination to further educate tourists and influence their behaviour at destinations, especially those in developing countries;

19. *incorporate* sustainable transportation principles in the planning and design of access and transportation systems, and encourage tour operators and the travelling public to make soft mobility choices.

B. To the private sector

20. *bear* in mind that for ecotourism businesses to be sustainable, they need to be profitable for all stakeholders involved, including the projects' owners, investors, managers and employees, as well as the communities and the conservation organizations of natural areas where it takes place;

21. *conceive, develop and conduct* their businesses minimizing negative effects on, and positively contributing to, the conservation of sensitive ecosystems and the environment in general, and directly benefiting and including local and indigenous communities;

22. *ensure* that the design, planning, development and operation of ecotourism facilities incorporates sustainability principles, such as sensitive site design and community sense of place, as well as conservation of water, energy and materials, and accessibility to all categories of population without discrimination;

23. *adopt* as appropriate a reliable certification or other systems of voluntary regulation, such as ecolabels, in order to demonstrate to their potential clients their adherence to sustainability principles and the soundness of the products and services they offer;

24. *cooperate* with governmental and non-governmental organizations in charge of protected natural areas and conservation of biodiversity, ensuring that ecotourism operations are practised according to the management plans and other regulations prevailing in those areas, so as to minimize any negative impacts upon them while enhancing the quality of the tourism experience and contribute financially to the conservation of natural resources;

25. *make* increasing use of local materials and products, as well as local logistical and human resource inputs in their operations, in order to maintain the overall authenticity of the ecotourism product and increase the proportion of financial and other benefits that remain at the destination. To achieve this, private operators should invest in the training of the local workforce;

26. *ensure* that the supply chain used in building up an ecotourism operation is thoroughly sustainable and consistent with the level of sustainability aimed at in the final product or service to be offered to the customer;

27. *work* actively with indigenous leadership and local communities to ensure that indigenous cultures and communities are depicted accurately and with respect, and that their staff and guests are well and accurately informed regarding local and indigenous sites, customs and history;

28. *promote* among their clients an ethical and environmentally conscious behaviour vis-à-vis the ecotourism destinations visited, such as by environmental education or by encouraging voluntary contributions to support local community or conservation initiatives;

29. *generate* awareness among all management and staff of local, national and global environmental and cultural issues through ongoing environmental education, and support the contribution that they and their families can make to conservation, community economic development and poverty alleviation;

30. *diversify* their offer by developing a wide range of tourist activities at a given destination and by extending their operations to different destinations in order to spread the potential benefits of ecotourism and to avoid overcrowding some selected ecotourism sites, thus threatening their long-term sustainability. In this regard, private operators are urged to respect, and contribute to, established visitor impact management systems of ecotourism destinations;

31. *create* and *develop* funding mechanisms for the operation of business associations or cooperatives that can assist with ecotourism training, marketing, product development, research and financing;

32. *ensure* an equitable distribution of financial benefits from ecotourism revenues between international, outbound and incoming tour operators, local service providers and local communities through appropriate instruments and strategic alliances;

33. *formulate* and *implement* company policies for sustainability with a view to applying them in each part of their operations.

C. To non-governmental organizations, community-based associations, academic and research institutions.

34. *provide* technical, financial, educational, capacity building and other support to ecotourism destinations, host community organizations, small businesses and the corresponding local authorities in order to ensure that appropriate policies, development and management guidelines, and monitoring mechanisms are being applied towards sustainability;

35. *monitor* and *conduct* research on the actual impacts of ecotourism activities upon ecosystems, biodiversity, local and indigenous cultures and the socio-economic fabric of the ecotourism destinations;

36. *cooperate* with public and private organizations ensuring that the data and information generated through research is channeled to support decision-making processes in ecotourism development and management;

37. *cooperate* with research institutions to develop the most adequate and practical solutions to ecotourism development issues.

D. To inter-governmental organizations, international financial institutions and development assistance agencies

38. *develop* and *assist* in the implementation of national and local policy and planning guidelines and evaluation frameworks for ecotourism and its relationships with biodiversity conservation, socio-economic development, respect of human rights, poverty alleviation, nature conservation and other objectives of sustainable development, and to intensify the transfer of such know-how to all countries.

Special attention should be paid to countries in a developing stage or least developed status, to small island developing States and to countries with mountain areas, considering that 2002 is also designated as the International Year of Mountains by the UN;

39. *build capacity* for regional, national and local organizations for the formulation and application of ecotourism policies and plans, based on international guidelines;

40. *develop or adopt, as appropriate,* international standards and financial mechanisms for ecotourism certification systems that take into account the needs of small and medium enterprises and facilitates their access to those procedures, and *support* their implementation;

41. *incorporate* multistakeholder dialogue processes into policies, guidelines and projects at the global, regional and national levels for the exchange of experiences between countries and sectors involved in ecotourism;

42. *strengthen* efforts in identifying the factors that determine the success or failure of ecotourism ventures throughout the world, in order to transfer such experiences and best practices to other nations, by means of publications, field missions, training seminars and technical assistance projects; UNEP, WTO and other international organizations should continue and expand the international dialogue after the Summit on sustainable tourism and ecotourism issues, for example by conducting periodical reviews of ecotourism development through international and regional forums;

43. *adapt* as necessary their financial facilities and lending conditions and procedures to suit the needs of micro-, small- and medium-sized ecotourism firms that are the core of this industry, as a condition to ensure its long term economic sustainability;

44. *develop* the internal human resource capacity to support sustainable tourism and ecotourism as a development sub-sector in itself and to ensure that internal expertise, research, and documentation are in place to oversee the use of ecotourism as a sustainable development tool;

45. *develop* financial mechanisms for training and capacity building, that takes into account the time and resources required to successfully enable local communities and indigenous peoples to participate equitably in ecotourism development.

E. To local and indigenous communities

In addition to all the references to local and indigenous communities made in the preceding paragraphs of this Declaration, (in particular para. 5, 8, 9 and 10 on page 2; para. 1 on page 3; in A 2 and 17; B 21 and 27; C 35; D 45) participants addressed the following recommendations to the local and indigenous communities themselves:

46. As part of a community vision for development, that may include ecotourism, *define* and *implement* a strategy for improving collective benefits for the community through ecotourism development including human, physical, financial, and social capital development, and improved access to technical information;

47. *strengthen, nurture* and *encourage* the community's ability to maintain and use traditional skills, particularly home-based arts and crafts, agricultural produce, traditional housing and landscaping that use local natural resources in a sustainable manner.

F. To the World Summit on Sustainable Development (WSSD)

48. *recognize* the need to apply the principles of sustainable development to tourism, and the exemplary role of ecotourism in generating economic, social and environmental benefits;

49. *integrate* the role of tourism, including ecotourism, in the outcomes expected at WSSD.

Québec City, Canada, 22 May 2002

ANNEX 1

WORLD ECOTOURISM SUMMIT

WTO/UNEP Summary of Regional Preparatory Conferences
to serve as
Discussion Paper for the World Ecotourism Summit

World Tourism Organization

UNEP

THEME A
ECOTOURISM POLICY AND PLANNING: THE SUSTAINABILITY CHALLENGE

**WTO/UNEP Summary of Regional Preparatory Conferences
to serve as
Discussion Paper for the World Ecotourism Summit**

Prepared by Ms. Pamela A. Wight

This report summarises the main outputs of the preparatory conferences leading up to the World Ecotourism Summit. The outputs discussed policies and planning at a range of scales, from international and national, to local and site specific. In addition, although there are 3 reports covering the other conference themes, a number of these themes were also addressed within some of the planning and policy development themed discussions, including; product development, regulations, costs and benefits, monitoring, and marketing. This seems to reinforce both the complexity of the subject and the interdependent nature of the themes.

1. ISSUES DISCUSSED

Key Overarching Issues and Challenges for Planning and Policy Development

A wide range of issues/challenges formed the major outputs of this Theme. In many cases, conference summaries seemed to direct outputs/recommendations to higher government levels. It is normally governments which develop most plans and policies, and it is these very plans and policies which impact the ecotourism operator or communities most (no conference summaries examined planning and policy development of ecotourism businesses or projects). Also, those at the "grass roots" tend to feel un-empowered, or less involved than they feel they should be. So it may be only natural for participants to address their recommendations upward to those public, private or non-governmental organizations who are in charge, or should be in charge of planning and policy development at the different levels.

A number of issues and challenges were of broad relevance across conference themes, and across most preparatory conferences. These tend to be within the mandate of *national* levels of government, and to involve multiple agencies, particularly those with protected areas mandates. Conferences indicated that to date, there has been little development and management of the community sector by authorities and managers of protected areas. In addition, strategies tend to be driven externally – so are not implemented because they are not developed and owned locally.

Need for Transboundary Management: It was recognised internationally and regionally, that ecotourism activities and resources do not necessarily adhere to administrative boundaries. This is a challenge for parks and protected areas. Ecosystems form a better basis for planning and policy making, yet are rarely the administrative units. Biological resources clearly cross administrative boundaries, but cultures also cross these boundaries, including indigenous cultures. The movement of visitors also crosses boundaries, and these flows are being impeded by administrative requirements in some regions (e.g., in CIS countries for both ship and land tourism). There is a need for better co-operation between countries sharing transboundary natural resources and protected areas to set up joint legislative and institutional frameworks that facilitate planning and management processes for conservation and tourism.

Lacking or Conflicting National Planning and Policy Objectives: This was probably the largest issue that emerged. It was specifically highlighted at every regional preparatory conference. Challenges are multi-layered, and · relate particularly to a lack of overall vision, a lack of integration of various sector/ministry policies, and frequently unspecified and unclear government department roles. The challenge is rooted in a lack of overarching sustainable development goals, perspectives, and mandates at senior government levels. The issue is exacerbated by intersecting responsibilities of many government ministries in developmental, planning and marketing issues related to ecotourism. Often, there are conflicting goals and mandates *within* individual ministries or agencies, which may lead to arbitrary or uncoordinated decision-making.

Inconsistent or Nonexistent Policy/Institutional Frameworks for Ecotourism: A common problem in many parts of the world is the lack of an institutional framework for the development of ecotourism, which is partly related to low recognition and value given to ecotourism. A number of regional conferences discussed the need for ecotourism policy frameworks. Policies are not consistent because they are generated within individual departments, or even within one arm of an agency, so policies further some agency objectives, without necessarily supporting the objectives of other agencies. This essentially means that sustainability objectives are not supported (e.g., some agencies have development mandates, while others have conservation mandates). Overarching policy frameworks are needed. In addition, some countries view ecotourism as one of many subsets of tourism, and do not therefore develop specific policy and institutional frameworks for ecotourism. All conferences felt it was senior Government's responsibility to develop national strategic plans and polices for ecotourism, while specific guidelines and tools are required at the regional or local level.

Need for Models of Successful Planning and Policy Development: Most conferences indicated that there was a lack of successful models related to: protected areas which function successfully as ecotourism products; practical planning and management tools; a range of policy-related options for local needs and circumstances; ways of integrating different agencies' and stakeholders' perspectives . The general need is for good examples of practical applications for ecotourism.

Lack of Fiscal Commitment: Every regional conference mentioned the lack of financial resources for: protected areas planning and management; community education, empowerment and training; research; and partnershipping activities. Budgets may reflect lack of ministry support or priorities, or politicians' priorities. Entrepreneurs also lack funding sources, particularly in difficult economic climates, (e.g., regions with developing economies, such as Andean and Meso-America,

African, Asian and Pacific regions). With a slightly different perspective, CIS countries feel that tourism should not be taxed more than other industries (e.g., through border fees, etc.) and the Arctic conference agreed.

Information is Lacking: Information is lacking for appropriate planning and development, and about trends in environmental and socio-economic implications of tourism and ecotourism. Key aspects identified as lacking included: quality research and analysis, resource inventories and other baseline data, and appropriate tools for planning and management of resources, impact, visitors, supply and demand (e.g., biodiversity /threat/ infrastructure/ services/ cultural resource inventories, visitor information and education techniques, use-intensity management, traffic management, niche market information, etc.).

Lack of Human Resource Capacity: There are many types of education, training and capacity building required, including of government staff, due to lack of appropriate expertise and to high staff turnover (e.g., increased planning skills needed). Capacity is required in individual entrepreneurs, particularly with respect to a broad range of business functions, knowledge of markets, hospitality, environmental issues, and the importance of socio-cultural perspectives and resource management. Capacity building is required among a range of community members with respect to such topics as hospitality, fulfilling visitor expectations, and how to become directly involved in ecotourism.

Land Tenure: A particularly important issue, especially in Africa, is the need to identify land tenure. It is difficult or impossible for indigenous peoples to develop land or facility based ecotourism if they cannot establish rights to the land. Legal mechanisms need to be in place for land rights to be recorded and established.

Empowerment of Local Communities Needed: Communities need to be able to take more control of the management of ecotourism, and should be involved in managing resources and benefits (directly and indirectly). Many regional conferences felt that ecotourism projects could be used to complement intensively-used destinations, reducing visitor pressures (which reduces disadvantages in other areas, e.g., Mountain areas, Europe). This included showing communities *how* they could be involved in planning and policy making processes, and the benefits that might accrue, as well as how to benefit: from ownership and control of ecotourism; from ecotourism planning and policy making initiatives; from galvanising local economies through a range of products; or from important conservation functions.

Enabling Participation of all Stakeholders: It was felt that planning and policy development is not carried out with much stakeholder involvement, and that often stakeholder participation tends to be unmeaningful. So strategies are often not implemented because they are not developed and "owned" locally. Meaningful involvement would lessen such concerns as maintaining authenticity of social systems, indigenous and other cultures. Not only should stakeholders be consulted, but planners and policy developers should develop creative and culturally appropriate ways to encourage a diversity of stakeholder input (e.g., obtaining advice from community workers, enabling verbal (vs. written) input, holding focussed discussions with diverse sub-groups, or working through school/ church/ sports/women's' groups, etc.).

2. RECOMMENDATIONS

Key Crosscutting Recommendations

Use National and International Transboundary Management Approaches

- International ecotourism planning and policies should be integrated across national and international boundaries, with respect to resource planning and management, and to visitor movement. Ecosystems are the appropriate management units, even if outside protected area boundaries

- Adjacent jurisdictions should develop mechanisms to ease border movements, particularly in CIS and adjacent countries (e.g., creating tourist cards to facilitate travel; relaxing visa procedures or currency/ exchange regulations; influencing airfare changes)

Governments Should Take Responsibility in Planning and Policy Development

- National level leadership and guidance should be demonstrated through consistent departmental and interdepartmental vision and objectives. Planning and policy development for ecotourism should be in the context of sustainable development objectives, and integrated with other economic, social and conservation activities (e.g., national policy co-ordination could be facilitated by Inter-Ministerial co-ordination committees at appropriate levels, and chaired by senior personnel)

- In some regional conferences, it was felt that ecotourism planning should be part of a larger sustainable tourism planning perspective, or integrated into other sectors' planning, while in other conferences it was recommended that specific corridors and areas be delimited for ecotourism (e.g., in the Meso-American conference, it was felt that protected area management plans should include clear goals for biological corridors and should analyse the potential of border areas to develop ecotourism corridors through land use plans.)

Plan Systematically for Protected Areas

- Protection of critical areas was considered a primary goal of protected areas management and fundamental to ecotourism planning and development. This reflects the view that management of *supply* (resources) should be the core concern. Visitor satisfaction (*demand*) should be considered, but in such a way as to support resource conservation rather than to be the primary driver of protected areas management. A protected areas planning framework should be developed for all countries/ regions, within the context of an overall vision

- Zoning is a strong tool that should be used in protected areas planning (including incorporating core areas and reserves, low and medium impact areas, and buffers). Zones should have strict regulations with enforcement, and infrastructure and facilities should be in peripheral areas

Formulate and Implement Policy and Planning Processes

- Some conferences recommended that public sector agencies, NGOs and other stakeholders involved in environmental and community matters establish co-operative agreements and set up an umbrella organisation to plan, regulate and monitor ecotourism activities

- Tourism planning and policy development should involve many sectors/ departments, particularly for protected areas (e.g., coastal area planning and management should include integrated strategies for air and water; ecotourism/tourism should be integrated into other sectors' planning and policy-making, using such tools as land use planning, transportation planning, town planning, infrastructure development, and socio-economic planning at all scales). Similarly, the tourism and culture sectors should collaborate (e.g., archaeological site conservation or presentation)

- Tourism planning (and protected area planning) should include clear goals and facilitation mechanisms for community development (e.g., community-owned micro-enterprise creation and development). Tourism policy development should ensure rules are not overly complex for either visitors or for communities

- The development of plans and polices for ecotourism should involve:
  - Vision and long-term perspectives at all levels
  - Appropriate policies for different scales, based on better information/data
  - A balance of voluntary and legislated regulation and activities
  - Definition of government's role with respect to ecotourism enterprises
  - Good integration of traditional mechanisms and institutions (already in place)

- Good examples of practical policies and plans should be disseminated, particularly those that demonstrate site-specific realities, monitoring, regulatory enforcement, and accountability.

Develop Appropriate Tools for Planning and Management

- International agencies should increase their collaboration and contribute to appropriate tools (e.g. developing policies, guidelines and codes of conduct. The World Tourism Organisation and other intergovernmental agencies could strengthen their role in sharing international experiences in ecotourism (e.g., producing publications, organizing forums, or identifying and disseminating best practices on ecotourism planning, policy development and management).

- Develop an inventory of tourism assets, together with appropriate research, including biodiversity, threats, and endangered species, should be part of ecotourism planning and development.

- Incorporate a range of appropriate tools in tourism planning and management (e.g., environmental assessments, vision development, determining acceptable numbers/types of visitors in protected areas, land use planning, appropriate places/timing of visitors, pricing policies, zoning mechanisms, facility controls, interpretive tools, guidelines and codes). Conditions of operation should be established for both marine and terrestrial operators.

Commit Adequate Financial Resources and Develop Appropriate Funding Mechanisms

- International funding agencies need to be encouraged to support ecotourism development projects. Funding mechanisms are also required for planning and co-operation at sub-regional levels.

- Government should view small-scale projects particularly favourably, through loans, grants, or other mechanisms, so as to ease/enable the entry of these enterprises into the marketplace. Support or subsidies should be done conditional on performance or impact monitoring related to ecotourism goals (e.g., defining targets, indicators, data collection, or biological conservation efforts). Such conditions of assistance should be appropriate to the size of the projects.

- Adequate core funding should be provided to protected areas, and government policies and regulatory mechanisms should mandate returning a portion of tourist revenues to conservation of the protected areas (rather than to general revenues).

- Create appropriate funding mechanisms to help sustain partnerships (e.g., NGOs could act as a conduit for funding projects or partnerships; or ecotourism projects eligible for international funding could be linked with international pro-poor and biodiversity agendas). It was suggested that regional research centres should be established for research and education on ecotourism, which would require a partnership approach.

Governments, Development Agencies, NGOs, Private Businesses and Others Should Build Local Capacity

- Capacity building should be a focus (especially in Africa and South America) to enable better *participation* in planning and policy development processes. Mechanisms should be developed to translate/explain the meaning and implications of proposed policies and plans to stakeholders.

- Training is the prime mechanism recommended to increase local employment, to add to product value, and to increase local business capabilities. It should be developed appropriately in terms of *content*, to reflect destination needs (e.g., CIS countries suggested accommodation management, guiding, languages). Similarly, the *manner* of delivery, training methods, and time frames, should be developed to suit the destination/recipient's cultural and learning style and needs (e.g., hands-on, or train-the-trainer).

- Private businesses should favour employing locals, and for this provide on-the-job training opportunities.

Build multi-Stakeholder Participation into Planning and Policy Development Processes

- Consulting a wide range of stakeholders (both inside and outside the destination) should be built into any planning, policy, or regulatory processes, to develop a sense of community and ownership. Consultation processes should be inclusive and transparent, with particular efforts to include the disadvantaged or the traditionally voiceless (e.g., indigenous groups, women, elders or youth). Planning should incorporate a range of benefits and goals for the community, and should ensure a bottom-up approach.

- The *manner* of consultation and participation mechanisms should be culturally appropriate to the target groups, and may vary within one planning or policy development process.

- Businesses and agencies should proactively contact stakeholders (e.g., cruise ships could initiate contact with stakeholders, to ensure measures are implemented to realise environmental protection and community benefits – Arctic conference). Similarly, central levels of government should initiate involving other levels.

Recommendations for Environmental Conservation

Conserve Material Resources at all Levels

- Plans and policies should ensure that resources are conserved and used more effectively. Use incentives, education, or other measures to encourage energy conservation (use of renewable sources); water conservation (and storage); waste management (3Rs: reduce, reuse, recycle); sustainable biological resource use; and reduced imported materials (especially into islands).

- In Mountain regions and Europe particularly, sustainable transportation should be built into destinations, vacation resorts, and other areas by planners and policy makers. Similarly, tour packagers should feature sustainable transportation in their products as a consumer benefit and a conservation approach.

Educate Communities about Biodiversity and Conservation

- Participatory processes should be used to educate local people about the value of biological and cultural diversity in ecotourism development, and on how they can both conserve and derive benefits from natural and cultural resources.

- Private companies should pursue voluntary initiatives with stakeholders to promote consumer awareness of environmentally and socially responsible tourism.

Manage Impacts

- Apply a range of approaches and tools for impact management. Carrying capacity studies were recommended to manage impact. Although many conferences focussed on this approach, they did not seem aware of the very large number of alternative tools to address problems of growth, impact or visitor activities and behaviour. Recommendations generally mentioned such specific and limited resource variables as water supply (in desert or island areas) or numbers of beds available locally, where carrying capacity (i.e., identifying the limiting variable threshold) might be a valuable tool.

- Curb unbridled growth through a range of mechanisms (other than a numbers limit). This was recommended as appropriate to deal with specific problems, such as managing group size, or group frequency, or other use-intensity management tools.

- Promote sustainable transportation through renting low-, or emission-free vehicles, street redesign, traffic speed regulation, cycling and rental spots, routes and information, and other non-motorised traffic modes. Companies should offer comprehensive sustainable transport packages, car free areas, and good intermodal transfer, through multi-stakeholder collaboration.

- Develop environmental or community standards/guidelines (e.g., for eco-accommodation in Asia-Pacific, or for activity limits in Andean South America).

Manage Visitors

- On the one hand, visitor management was recommended to reduce/manage impact, while on the other, it was recommended that protected areas or even countries/regions not have such complex rules that visitation is deterred. Demand management (in terms of type, numbers, concentration, and spread) was recommended. Thus some areas might be developed as tourist *nodes* or compact tourist destinations to develop a critical mass and increase development feasibility; while other areas may encourage more visitor *spread* (e.g., to disadvantaged rural or mountain areas). A related recommendation was identification of appropriate markets using alliances of NGOs to perform focus group and other survey work.

- Use economic policies to manage visitors (e.g., entrance fee policies to help channel seasonal traffic, lower stress on infrastructure, and help pay for services offered).

- Use information and education as strong management tools (e.g., via signposts, alternative routes, different entry points, information centres, interpretive centres, guides, interpretation).

- Use interpretation as both a visitor education and management tool. To increase interpretation capabilities, introduce ecotourism interpretation programs in universities, tourism and hotel schools, tourism training and capacity building programs.

Recommendations for Economic Development

Build Small Business Capabilities and Provide Incentives for Sustainable Practices

- Strengthen small and medium sized (SME) and micro enterprises, to position them for success (particularly recommended in Africa). Such training programs might include business start-up, hospitality, investment, entrepreneurial activities, management, accommodations management, market analysis, marketing and sustainability. Other types of training programs should include tour guiding, interpretation, and responses to specific local needs

- Develop incentives for small ecotourism businesses that ensure environmental protection and local sustainability (e.g., through financial mechanisms, provision of exclusive access to key areas, provision of guarantees or long-term leases, adjustment of conditions of operation, sharing research findings, joint marketing incentives, etc.)

Provide Government and other Support for Community Level Ecotourism

- Infrastructural support should be provided (adjacent to parks and protected areas or within designated zones) that assist local communities in ecotourism development (e.g., signage, accommodation, routes, transportation, telecommunication, electricity, water, waste and sewage treatment facilities, etc.).

- Build on existing subsistence or economic activities. Ecotourism activities should be used to support development of disadvantaged areas and alleviate poverty (e.g., on islands, or in rural poor areas) through planning and decision-making. Means could include resource use/development policies, affirmative action policies, capacity building, and focussed education. Micro-credit programs should be developed to assist small scale enterprises. Some conferences recommended that local ecotourism businesses with community involvement should be favoured over multi-national tourism companies.

- The role of governments should be more as a facilitator of ecotourism operations and businesses developing public-private co-operation mechanisms, rather than being operators themselves. This allows government to develop multistakeholder frameworks for monitoring and regulatory activities, and enables entrepreneurial capabilities to flourish.

Educate Destinations about Sustainable Means to Increase Economic Benefits

- The misconception that increased visitation is the way to increase economic benefits is in part responsible for some of the negative impacts of tourism. Inform stakeholders about other ways to increase economic benefits (e.g., by retaining the same visitor for longer, or providing opportunities for visitors to spend more, such as by identifying more festivals, enhancing cultural tours with add-ons, expanding local crafts, enhancing packages with additional activities or opportunities to induce visitors to purchase longer tours).

Recommendations for Social and Cultural Benefits

Enhance Use of Heritage Resources

- By protecting and rehabilitating historic/heritage buildings, monuments, and structure through policy, and use them for tourism purposes (e.g. accommodation, catering, information centre, exhibitions, etc).

Involve Communities and Give Ownership

- Encourage community involvement in social and cultural programming, to provide direct economic and cultural benefits, as well as to enhance visitor experiences and authenticity.

- Involve communities and all operators in monitoring impacts, or other feedback requirements.

- Obtain community input about traditional and cultural activities, to determine the activities of value and sustain these via planning and policies, and to preserve critical elements of a culture (e.g., aboriginal land based economic activities).

Education and Awareness Building

- Education and awareness-building need to be directed to the full range of stakeholders, and should address all elements of sustainability – conservation and protection; economic feasibility; and socio-cultural benefits of ecotourism. Community awareness campaigns are needed about ecotourism regulations and policies, and training about tourism pros and cons, hospitality, how to obtain increased added value from visitors, and how to manage and take control of tourism locally. Obtain leverage by focussing initially on community decision-makers.

- Ensure that governments, agencies, tour operators, and outside companies know that they have some responsibilities/opportunities in preventing/resolving certain problems which communities may have (problems which originate outside the communities, since locals are often only in control of internal elements of their current condition).

- NGOs should develop more short-term planning processes that could be transferred effectively to communities for their future use.

Recommendations for Multi-Stakeholder Participation

Joint Ventures

- Facilitation of community level joint ventures should occur, particularly with the private sector. Examples suggested in preparatory conference summaries include: community co-management of protected areas to enable community-developed products with protected areas agencies; strategic alliances between private businesses and local communities to enable benefit-sharing such as through providing local goods or services; non-governmental organisation support for and assistance with community-level projects; arrangements between inbound operators and destinations to include sustainable package elements in their offerings, such as sustainable transportation. Support for joint ventures could be built into planning (e.g., the development of guidelines for agreements between communities and all other stakeholders) or into policy initiatives (e.g., through incentives, subsidies, demonstrations, training programs, etc.).

3. POINTS FOR FURTHER DEBATE

Many of the preparatory conference planning and policy development recommendations summarised above identify issues, challenges and problems in ecotourism planning and policy, but they don't define specific solutions for most of them. The recommendations are often directed at senior levels of government, especially with respect to coordinating activities both horizontally (between agencies), and vertically (from national to community levels). Discussions at the World Ecotourism Summit may wish to consider the fact that there is a need for good practices to be highlighted in this area, as well as specific tools to enable appropriate implementation.

Suggested topics for discussion might include:

- The need to manage impact or to limit tourists, and how to do this, is a difficult issue. More specific discussion or examples of multiple approaches and mechanisms would be useful (e.g., using a range of voluntary, educational, and incentive-based approaches, as well as the conventional regulatory mechanisms)

- The approach of participatory and adaptive (co)-management could be a fruitful line of discussion

- Practical ways to integrate ecotourism planning into broader regional or local development policies and plans. This could involve how to encourage diverse agencies to co-operate; how to integrate policies into other community, regional, or enterprise support initiatives; or how government should be involved in a range of activities from support for new ecotourism initiatives to research activities

- There is a need for good practices to be highlighted in development of legislative, regulatory and policy tools, which address community-based problems

- Practical suggestions for how communities can take control of their future

- While discussions focussed strongly on communities, the needs and perspectives of indigenous peoples were not always differentiated from those of mainstream communities. How to involve indigenous minorities meaningfully in planning and policy development could be a fruitful discussion

- Those mechanisms which achieve *both* environmental and socio-cultural benefits could be explored

- How to constructively involve those who are related to ecotourism activities and part of current problems/solutions, but are not necessarily aware of this, should be addressed, since all players have useful contributions to solutions

- How to involve politicians, persuade them of the benefits of a more integrated approach, and to make them care about environmental and socio-cultural values, and about ecotourism

- There is a need for more examples of good ecotourism policy-making and planning, and for practical examples of the implementation of plans and policies, especially those which demonstrate a good balance between centralised policies and site-specific realities, and those which successfully demonstrate accountability and monitoring

THEME B
REGULATION OF ECOTOURISM:
INSTITUTIONAL RESPONSIBILITIES AND FRAMEWORKS

**WTO/UNEP Summary of Regional Preparatory Conferences
to serve as
Discussion Paper for the World Ecotourism Summit**

Prepared by Mr. Francesc Giró

Introduction

A number of issues were discussed at the different preparatory conferences in relation to the need to monitor and regulate ecotourism, and stressing the need and importance of evaluating progress towards sustainability. There is a wide range of situations, depending on which part of the world we are talking about. In some areas ecotourism is well developed, the governments have set up regulations, a number of certification systems are available and there is only a need to evaluate if there is a real progress towards sustainability. On the other hand, there are regions where ecotourism is just appearing, there is a lack of institutional support and regulations are inexistent. In between these two extreme cases, there are a number of varied situations in the different continents, with different needs and with one common issue, which is the development of ecotourism.

WTO has been devoting a great effort to the development and dissemination of methodologies for the identification and use of sustainability indicators in tourism development. The WTO publication *"What Tourism Managers Need to Know - A Practical Guide to the Development and Use of Indicators of Sustainable Tourism"* defines a set of core indicators, which would be of potential use in all destinations, together with supplementary indicators for specific types of destinations (e.g., coastal resorts, small islands, eco-, cultural and community tourism sites). Another very interesting development related to evaluation is The Global Reporting Initiative, set up by UNEP and other institutions, which is producing specific indicators for reporting on the activity of Tour Operators, within the UNEP/WTO/UNESCO Tour Operator Initiative for Sustainable Tourism Development.

1. ISSUES DISCUSSED

Institutional framework

A common problem in many parts of the world is the lack of an institutional framework for the development of ecotourism. Besides that, in many countries the presence of many governmental ministries who have intersecting responsibilities regarding the developmental, planning and marketing issues relating to ecotourism, can become a problem since such bodies have contradicting agendas: balancing development of tourism (in this case ecotourism) and conservation of the natural and cultural assets. The need to develop umbrella mechanisms that allow such bodies to work successfully together in order to create the balance necessary for the development of ecotourism was also stressed. In some areas there was an agreement in the fact that Governmental commitment to conservation and ecotourism development is one of the most important factors for operational success. Since the natural environment is the primary attraction in many ecotourism destinations, it is imperative that public, private and non-governmental organizations co-operate in regulating the industry and enforcing the institutional framework. In some areas such as Europe in general, and the Mediterranean countries, the situation is different. Institutional frameworks are in place to guarantee proper development of ecotourism. However, in general there is confusion between ecotourism and other kinds of sustainable tourism and also the situation and real potential for ecotourism is very different depending on which country we are talking about.

Regulation

There has been a general agreement in pointing Ecotourism Certification and regulation as key factors of evaluation with a view to sustainability. An important point discussed was the need for public-private sector cooperation with a view to establishing policies, strategies and regulations relative to sustainable tourism development. Emphasis was made on how important it is to consult with all the players in protected areas, including the administrative bodies on the matter of regulating ecotourism flows. In desert countries where borders very often have nothing to do with geographical limits, there was an agreement in the fact that regulations for ecotourism in protected areas should be extended beyond the frontiers of the neighbour countries. In some cases there was some resistance against the definition of regulations and it was suggested that a better approach would be to establish guidelines, and only after, a next step could be to transform a list of optional guidelines into obligatory regulations. In general, it was recognised that a variety of regulations need to be developed such as codes of conduct, guidelines and so on, together with legal regulations that help reduce negative impacts. Finally, in many cases there was agreement on the need and interest and very often there was not more regulation because of a lack of financial and technical resources.

Certification and labelling

In continents where ecotourism is well developed, one of the main issues that were discussed was certification and labelling. The experiences analysed during these conferences confirmed the need for basic guidelines, which should be adapted by each country to meet its specific conditions. Attention was drawn to the risk of certification being used as a non-tariff barrier by external buyers, which would have a particularly detrimental effect on small businesses.
Quality labels such as The European Charter for sustainable tourism in protected areas are very useful tools for helping such areas/destinations and tourism business/enterprises to define their sustainable tourism strategy by means of a strategic and participatory approach. Such labels aim to ensure the development and management of tourism in protected areas in a sustainable way, taking into account the needs of the environment (efficient protection), local residents (economic benefits and living standards improvements), local business (higher profits due to a high

selling value of the labelled area) and visitors (high quality tourism experience). Labelling was agreed to be one of the ways to regulate ecotourism. In countries where ecotourism and certification are less developed, there was some resistance to it, with the belief that small-scale ecotourism products could not reach the standards.

Definition of evaluation and monitoring criteria

There are few examples of monitoring of ecotourism in order to evaluate progress towards sustainability. Communities need to identify what needs they have, the ways in which tourism can meet those needs and the delivery of those needs then need to be time lined in order to define evaluation and monitoring criteria. In a number of preparatory meetings, there was an agreement in the fact that there is a need for some kind of monitoring and evaluation of the degree of success of ecotourism projects, which can be used as case studies in the region to show, in a practical manner, the benefits of ecotourism development both for local people and for conservation.

The situation is very different in each country but the experiences presented have shown that there is a need for basic guidelines for ecotourism development that can then be adapted to the context of each country. Evaluation and accreditation where found to be important tools for the improvement of ecotourism products and also for making easier the process of progress monitoring.

Identification of indicators

The identification of indicators and its difficulty was a subject of debate in a number of meetings. One of the indicators used was the collective welfare of the community, as it covers both community and individual benefits from ecotourism. One important point was to find out what proportion of income is going to individuals, households and to community projects and then how to monitor this. It was pointed out how important it is to secure information about community benefits from ecotourism. Sometimes the indicators set by governments are difficult to use, particularly where the indicators suggested by government are intrusive, such as the monitoring of household earnings in rural communities, which can have constraints. Other indicators are more suitable, in that they are in the public domain: for example the number of bicycles, better housing, ability to send children to school etc.

Another possible approach shown was to measure household income and other community indicators from the demand side. Surveys of tourist expenditure can reveal a great deal about community benefits without having to investigate household earnings in rural communities. It is possible to discover from tourists what they have been spending and where, and from this information to make good estimates of the amount of money flowing into local communities from tourism. Similarly it is a relatively easy matter to identify from the tourism industry the amount of money that is being spent in the local community. It was finally pointed out that performance indicators needed to be determined and agreed in the design phase of programmes and projects and to be related to clear development objectives.

2. RECOMMENDATIONS

Regulation of ecotourism

- Move gradually from optional guidelines and simple codes of conduct, into obligatory regulations.

- Legal regulations may be necessary to help reduce the negative impacts of ecotourism.

- Governments should provide leadership, coordinate planning and set the legislative and regulatory framework needed for successful ecotourism.

- Establishment of suitable legal frameworks underpinned by effective tools for controlling and monitoring ecotourism activities, along with other instruments, such as certification and accreditation, which contribute to improving the quality of ecotourism products.

- In order to become credible, certification processes must be transparent, readily understandable and broadly publicized, in addition, to which they should be subject to periodic updates.

- It is essential to consult with all the players in nature parks and with the administrative bodies involved on the matter of regulating ecotourism flows, safeguarding threatened sites and training guides while also creating awareness.

- Development of International, Regional and National Policies in order to address issues affecting the development of ecotourism. They should include guidelines, codes of conduct and best practices that define ecotourism.

- Establishment of management plans in protected areas which include sustainable development of tourism, zoning, codes of conduct, and land use planning, etc, in order to regulate ecotourism activities.

Labelling

- The enforcement of control mechanisms and monitoring of eco-quality has to be done with the participation of all stakeholders involved.

- Accommodation classification should include an ecolabel or eco-certification scheme in order to improve sustainability performance of accommodation facilities in ecotourism and provide consumers with reliable expectations and advice before booking.

- Involve all stakeholders in the acceptance and use of all tools for achieving sustainability in eco-tourism (eco-labels, brands, indicators, carrying capacity assessment, even the legislation).

- Compliance with general tourism regulations and codes should be stricter in the case of ecotourism, combining supervision and monitoring, with awareness raising campaigns among business people and tourists, training of service suppliers and possibly sanctions against those who do not comply.

- The participatory design and implementation of a voluntary certification system of sustainability of ecotourism activities should be promoted.

Monitoring

- The monitoring of the benefits of ecotourism for the local community should not be solely based on monetary indicators but also on socio-cultural factors such as infrastructure development, education and health services, as well as the community's changed perception of its natural assets and their conservation.

- It is also important to measure changes in the level of awareness and acceptance of conservation in particular communities over periods of time.

- There needs to be transparency and independent review of the performance of projects in their contributions to both conservation and local communities.

- Setting targets and monitoring performance against the targets is important in assessing the scale of the achievement. This requires a record keeping system e.g. numbers of visitors, visitor satisfaction and expenditure etc.

- Effective monitoring needs defining targets, which should be achieved in a certain time period (e.g. the number of tourists, ratios between modes of transport in terms of arrivals, water purification, reduction of noise and traffic, raising local generated income of people, employment etc.).

- Indicators to measure performance and impacts should be defined. The range of indicators should include the social, ecological and economic development. They should cover those elements which are most crucial for local sustainability (e.g. water, area, bio-diversity, transport, employment, local income, local quality of life, security, crime);

- There should be continuous data collection involving business and tourists (e.g. questionnaires); the involvement of all stakeholders in the monitoring process and monitoring institutions; and regular revision of the local ecotourism strategy taking account of the results of the monitoring process.

- Local governments need to strengthen their technical capabilities to be able to monitor the performance of commercial tourism companies and of tourists within protected and non-protected mountain areas.

- National subsidies and support for local projects and strategies must ensure that monitoring is a prerequisite of the projects, and that adequate financial resources are devoted to the monitoring process after the life of the aid programme.

- NGOs should be involved in monitoring progress, since they can play an important role in order to guarantee the benefits of ecotourism development, both for local people and for the conservation of the diverse natural resources of the region. At the same time, taking charge of these operational activities allows a high level of control and monitoring of ecotourism.

- Monitoring systems should be established in order to evaluate the economic, social and environmental impact of ecotourism.

- Local communities should be supported so that they could take part in the process of monitoring the impact of ecotourism.

Evaluation

Evaluation systems for sustainability of tourism have to choose indicators and criteria for an assessment scheme that balances between indicators for state of society and state of environment, socio-economic driving forces, socio-economic and environmental pressures and driving forces and indicators for institutional frames. Such evaluations should be done and published on a regular basis, allowing for voluntary benchmarking of destinations.

3. ISSUES FOR FURTHER DEBATE

- The reduction of the uncontrolled launch of pseudo-eco-labels. Creation of an "umbrella" eco-brand by joining tourism, environment and consumer associations.
- Extend Certification to other aspects of ecotourism activity such as service quality and the participation of local communities in the management of ecotourism and the benefits thereof, besides environmental issues.
- To establish Certification on a voluntary basis or as an instrument to complement the regulation of ecotourism ventures.
- The certification of ecotourism products should pave the way for benefits and incentives for certified companies.
- To explore easily accessible funding formulae to cover the cost of international certification systems which makes them inaccessible to small businesses.
- Ecotourism certifiers must be guided by social criteria geared to facilitating the integration of small businesses at preferential rates and through technical contributions or the promotion of collective certification alternatives.
- Financially sound NGOs should shoulder the role of a certification body at a cost more affordable for local entrepreneurs.
- Local certification initiatives must be extended with a view to promoting the creation of regional networks, which could in turn be recognized (accredited) by international systems.

- In the light of the proliferation of "eco-labels" and certification systems, steps must be taken to promote the establishment of an equivalent system or certification based on international parameters, which involves the concept of accreditation.
- Certain laws and regulations within protected areas should be extended beyond their frontiers.
- To promote a constructive public-private sector relationship. Private sector operators should take responsibility for the economic, social and environmental impact of their activities.
- The private sector should be included in the process of designing regulations.
- Establishment of an international award scheme for ecotourism destinations, associated with the UNESCO world heritage site designation, as an incentive for improved ecotourism planning and management.
- Most of the existing concepts for eco-labels, brands and certification systems have to be enlarged by social and cultural aspects to reach the aims of sustainable ecotourism.
- To establish legally binding instruments for the implementation of sustainable ecotourism and avoidance of non-sustainable forms of tourism for sensitive areas, especially mountain regions, if the implementation is accompanied by specific regional strategies and measures.
- The development of legislative frameworks at the regional level should be supported, because they can positively influence sustainability issues, including the promotion of eco-tourism and similar types of tourism harmonized with the environment.
- Some countries have suggested that strict regulations for ecotourism at an international level should be avoided, while guidelines are acceptable.
- Consideration of the obligatory introduction of certification systems for ecotourism facilities and operations, at least at regional and possibly at worldwide level, to guarantee that the quality provided is consistent with the principles of sustainability.
- One proposal was made in order to raise financial resources from visitors in order to fund conservation and management the natural environment and cultural heritage, as in many countries in Asia this proved to be one of the problems limiting the proper development of ecotourism.

THEME C
PRODUCT DEVELOPMENT, MARKETING AND PROMOTION OF ECOTOURISM: FOSTERING SUSTAINABLE PRODUCTS AND CONSUMERS

**WTO/UNEP Summary of Regional Preparatory Conferences
to serve as
Discussion Paper for the World Ecotourism Summit**

Prepared by Dr. Richard Denman

Abstract

This report by Dr Richard Denman, one of four experts appointed by WTO and UNEP for the World Ecotourism Summit, summarises key themes, issues and recommendations for product development and marketing of ecotourism, arising from the preparatory conferences. It starts by listing some challenges to be faced, especially by small projects which find it hard to reach markets. Priority areas for action are identified as:

- Creating the right structures for working together
- Relating products to markets from the outset
- Paying attention to all aspects of product quality
- Providing relevant support for communities and enterprises
- Strengthening the promotion of ecotourism messages and products.

The report presents broad recommendations in each of these areas and provides a list of key topics for further debate at the Summit.

Product Development, Marketing and Promotion of Ecotourism: Summary Report

This report is a summary of the main conclusions of the preparatory conferences held in 2001 and 2002 in advance of the World Ecotourism Summit. The report covers issues relating to product development, marketing and promotion of ecotourism, which is the third of the four Summit themes. Parallel reports have been prepared on the other themes: policy and planning; regulation; and monitoring.

1. ISSUES DISCUSSED

The context of ecotourism development and marketing

During the preparatory conferences many case studies were presented of ecotourism projects from around the world, established by a wide range of private, voluntary and public bodies. Each had its own story to tell. Lessons learned from this practical experience were debated and discussed and then reflected in the conference reports.

Looking across all the regions, although there are notable differences in the type of ecotourism experience on offer, in the level of resources available and the challenges faced, there are striking similarities in the objectives behind ecotourism development and in the issues involved in establishing and maintaining sustainable products. This gives legitimacy to drawing global conclusions from the Summit.

There is still great variation in the understanding of what constitutes an ecotourism product. While it is broadly accepted that we are talking about a nature-based experience that is managed in a sustainable way, many presentations covered other types of product and wider issues of sustainable tourism. There are regional differences here: a strong focus on wildlife and wilderness is apparent in the Americas and Africa, while in Asia there is particular interest in the associated cultural dimension and in Europe ecotourism is often linked to rural tourism and landscapes shaped by man. A common thread is the concept of a product that provides the visitor with an authentic understanding of the area's natural and cultural heritage, and involves and benefits local people.

In all regions, the purpose behind the development of ecotourism products can be equated with sustainable development objectives. In some situations the underlying motive may be to benefit conservation, through generating more resources or providing an alternative, more environmentally sustainable, local economic base. Elsewhere, the motivation may be more to do with diversifying the economy and the tourism market, or tackling rural poverty. Many products are developed for a multitude of reasons. In all cases, the principles behind successful product development and marketing are similar.

Although there may be similarities in objectives and principles, the starting point and individual circumstances of each project may be vastly different. Current levels of visitation, inherent attractiveness of the area, accessibility and infrastructure, ecological sensitivity, local skills base, and community structure and aspirations, will vary. These differences exist within all regions as well as between them. Therefore each individual project needs to be very carefully assessed and planned.

Key challenges and priorities

The preparatory conferences have demonstrated that in all regions of the world there are many excellent ecotourism projects delivering positive benefits to local communities and the conservation of the environments in which they are located, as well as a fulfilling experience for visitors. However, there are also many challenges for product development and marketing.

Too many products fail

There are examples in most regions of ecotourism products which have failed through lack of profitability, or are likely to do so when donor support is no longer available. Often these are community-based and perhaps started primarily for conservation reasons. A common problem is lack of market response and poor feasibility assessment and business planning.

Small enterprises and community-based products find it hard to reach markets

Cost effective promotion is a challenge for many ecotourism enterprises because of their isolation, small size and lack of resources and skills.

The quality of visitor experience and environmental performance can be inconsistent

Excellent ecotourism products are to be found in every region, but the sector can be let down by products with an insufficient quality of service or environmental management. Sometimes the problem may lie in the surrounding destination, its infrastructure and planning control, rather than in the ecotourism project itself.

Visitors to natural areas could contribute more to conservation and local communities

Many natural environments, including protected areas, are already receiving significant visitor numbers. The challenge and opportunity for product development and marketing is to stimulate more visitor spending per head, minimise leakage away from the local area, reduce environmental impact and increase support for conservation.

The public is still relatively unaware of, or unresponsive to, sustainability issues

Despite the growth in demand for nature-based tourism, only a small proportion of travellers, including those from specialist niche markets, appear to be specifically seeking out sustainable products. Many suppliers and host communities are also still not sufficiently aware of sustainability issues.

In the face of these challenges, the following priority areas for action can be identified:

• **Creating the right structures for working together**
  All the preparatory conferences stressed the need for stakeholders to work together on the development and marketing of ecotourism products. None of the successful case study examples were operating in isolation.

• **Relating products to markets from the outset**
  A common call has been to relate supply to demand, with a better understanding of markets and how to reach them.

• **Paying attention to all aspects of product quality**
  Attention to detail is needed in product design and management in order to meet market interests and sustainability objectives.

- **Providing relevant support for communities and enterprises**
  Small enterprises and local communities require technical and financial assistance, which is locally delivered and tailored to their needs.

- **Strengthening the promotion of ecotourism messages and products**
  More can be done globally and locally to promote the concept of ecotourism and help products reach their customers.

The remainder of this report looks at the main points arising from the preparatory conferences within each of these areas.

2. RECOMMENDATIONS

Structures and relationships for product development and marketing

Local communities, private sector enterprises, NGOs, local authorities and protected areas, national governments and international agencies all have a role to play in ecotourism development and marketing.

- **Address local community needs and opportunities.** All preparatory conferences have emphasised the importance of working with local and indigenous communities in determining the level and type of tourism development in their area and in encouraging individual entrepreneurship, community-based enterprise and employment opportunities for local people.

- **Recognise the key role of private sector businesses.** Fostering and working with successful private sector operations, encouraging and helping them to meet a combination of commercial, social and environmental objectives, has proved to be a sound strategy. It is important to strengthen links between private operators and local communities. International and incoming tour operators have an important role to play, not only in promoting ecotourism but also in advising on product development and the overall quality of a destination, relating this to customer requirements.

- **Strengthen networking between small enterprises and projects.** There was a frequent call for small ecotourism enterprises to work together, to strengthen their marketing outreach and encourage common standards. Examples vary from associations of village community ecotourism products in a number of Asian and African countries, to branded small farm based accommodation enterprises in Europe with central booking services. Two conferences put forward the concept of local clusters of ecotourism initiatives, thereby establishing a critical mass of product in one area which would provide a composite visitor experience, be more able to attract business and justify investment in supporting infrastructure.

- **Recognise protected areas as focal points for ecotourism products and marketing.** Often parks and other protected areas provide the main draw for visitors, creating an opportunity for local communities to gain economic benefit through the provision of facilities and services. The relationship between protected

97

area authorities and local communities and tourism enterprises can be a critical one. There are various examples of stakeholder groups or wider liaison forums attached to national or nature parks, enabling the park to influence standards, marketing messages and new projects, while also supporting and coordinating enterprises and reflecting their needs. The quality of a park's own facilities and services, and the relationship between visitor management and conservation policies, is obviously of major importance in its own right.

- **Increase support from national and local government** for product development and marketing of ecotourism. Priorities may include infrastructure improvement, including sustainable transport, and featuring ecotourism more strongly in destination and thematic promotional campaigns.

Understanding ecotourism markets

The preparatory conferences recognised the importance of a realistic market assessment when developing and promoting ecotourism products.

- **Use more market research.** There was a general agreement that not enough is known about ecotourism markets and more research is needed. This has been partly addressed by WTO studies of the ecotourism market in the seven main generating countries, prepared for the International Year and presented at most preparatory conferences. These studies used quite a narrow definition of ecotourism, characterised by its size, impacts, educational components as well as visitor interest in nature and culture in natural areas. Results have pointed to this being a small niche market yet strongly growing. Although specialist tour operators are important in this market, the majority of ecotourists are individual travellers making their own arrangements.

- **Take a broad view of the market, recognising different segments.** Many individual enterprises and destinations have suggested that they are attracting a range of different types of visitor, including people enjoying an ecotourism experience as part of a more general holiday, domestic tourists and schools groups as well as more specialist nature tourism niche markets. More informed market segmentation will enable products and promotional strategies to be adapted to different expectations and requirements.

- **Study current visitor flows and local market conditions.** The pattern and distribution of tourism demand in the area, the performance of comparable operations, and the strengths and weaknesses of the location, should be carefully assessed, before product development takes place.

Key components of ecotourism products

The composition of ecotourism products should vary in order to satisfy different market segments and local conditions. However, some general priorities were identified at the preparatory conferences.

- **Address quality, authenticity and security**. Throughout the preparatory conferences, the importance of these three attributes was underlined. Quality does not necessarily mean luxury, but attention to detail and understanding customer needs. Authenticity is about meeting a visitor aspiration of 'seeing the real thing' while respecting the sensitivities of local communities and environments. Security is about visitor safety, perceived and real, but can also be applied to wider issues of reliability.

- **Give top priority to the interpretation of nature and culture**. The most essential component of an ecotourism product is the inherent quality of the landscape and wildlife. The WTO market studies confirmed this as the main visitor motivation, but closely followed by the opportunity to meet local people and experience cultural traditions and lifestyles. Ecotourism is distinguished by providing an experience that is both educative and enjoyable. Quality of interpretation is of paramount importance; within this, the value of good local guides, who know their subject and how to put it over, has been strongly emphasised.

- **Design and manage service facilities to maximise sustainability**. Although not the driving force in an ecotourism offer, accommodation, catering, and opportunities to make purchases are essential components of the product. There is a whole host of planning, design and management issues here that affect viability, environmental impact, enterprise and employment opportunities for local people, value retained in the local economy and the quality of the visitor experience. Case studies presented during the preparatory conferences have demonstrated a wealth of good practice in this area and a growing body of knowledge internationally, on topics such as: eco-lodge design and management; village based accommodation and homestay programmes; use of local produce and traditional dishes; and handicraft production and sales.

- **Address destination as well as individual product issues.** Successful and sustainable product development in ecotourism also needs to take account of infrastructure, environmental management and visitor services in the destination as a whole. For example, the need for more sustainable transport options to and within the destination was stressed at the European preparatory conference.

- **Relate ecotourism to sustainable activity tourism, where appropriate**. Although ecotourism is clearly distinguished from activity tourism, it is apparent that some ecotourists are looking for activities such as hiking or trail riding to complement the product offer. This appears to be particularly true in mountain areas, in regions like Europe and Central Asia. In maritime locations, such as small island states, making activities like diving and yachting more environmentally sustainable was seen as an issue for ecotourism. Three conferences also raised the controversial question of the relationship between hunting and ecotourism, recognising that this activity, when carefully controlled, can provide resources for wildlife management and raise the perceived value of certain species within local communities.

Technical support for communities and enterprises

In all regions there is a recognised need for local communities and small enterprises to receive relevant technical support to assist product development and marketing.

- **Provide relevant local training**. Locally available skills training is required, covering guiding, environmental management, customer care, catering, languages, promotion and information technology. It has also been emphasised that people from indigenous and local communities should be supported in taking up management positions in ecotourism. Capacity building of this kind has been assisted by governments, NGOs, donor agencies, educational institutions and the private sector, often working fruitfully in partnership. The importance of developing such programmes with local people and private enterprises, to ensure they are tailored to need and have local ownership, has been stressed. Some projects have demonstrated the advantage of including local government officials and NGOs in training programmes.

- **Encourage people to look together at the local resource and at other projects.** A number of conferences pointed to the value of local study tours to raise people's awareness of conservation issues and the opportunities of ecotourism. Projects were also presented where the stimulation and sound practical knowledge came from visits to successful ecotourism projects elsewhere. There may be opportunities to develop more twinning and multi-lateral links between projects.

- **Provide targeted, accessible financial assistance.** The important contribution of micro-credit and small grant schemes for ecotourism was demonstrated by a number of projects, and there has been a call for more financial support that is within the reach of local entrepreneurs, including resources for marketing. However, one preparatory conference emphasised the need to avoid developing ecotourism products that will remain dependent on public subsidy in the long term.

Promoting ecotourism messages and products

In general the preparatory conferences have called for more promotion of ecotourism, while recognising that the level of promotion of any one location should be determined by its carrying capacity and take account of the views of the local community.

- **Promote ecotourism as a concept**. There is a particular desire to see more active promotion of the principles and values of ecotourism, to recipient communities and to the travelling public. There is a need for a stronger international campaign to make tourists aware of both the harmful and the beneficial impacts of their activities, and how this depends on their travel choice. This could go beyond simply the generic message, with promotional support for relevant certification schemes and for activities such as donating to conservation causes in destinations visited. One conference emphasised the need to focus on the promotion of ecotourism to young people, as a receptive audience and the travellers of the future.

• **Grasp the significant opportunity presented by the Internet.** The Internet has had a major impact as a medium for promoting individual ecotourism products and the considerable potential it presents is widely recognised. It lends itself well to the ecotourism market, which is particularly responsive to up to date, detailed information and reports from previous travellers. A cautionary note was sounded about the lack of consumer trust in making bookings through the Internet, but this is being overcome as specific sites and brands are becoming better known. The advent of IT based Destination Management Systems will help to link demand to supply more efficiently.

• **Use a range of techniques and partners.** Despite the growth in Internet use, there was general recognition that ecotourism products should continue to use a range of promotional tools in their marketing, including working with specialist media and tour operators. There was a strong call for national and local tourist organisations to become more actively engaged in promoting ecotourism themes and products, in their publications and through travel fairs and familiarisation trips.

• **Provide comprehensive and educative information at all stages**. The detail and accuracy of information supplied to visitors in advance of their stay is particularly important in this sector. Ecotourists need to know what to expect. As well as covering travel details and facilities, this should include information on the ecology and culture of the area and how to respect it. Likewise, the quality of information supplied during their stay, for example by hosts, protected area authorities or local tour operators, can greatly affect the visitors' experience and their impact on the local community.

• **Create loyal ambassadors.** Almost all conferences stressed the importance of 'word of mouth' recommendation as the most potent form of marketing. Providing visitors with a quality experience, getting feedback from them and maintaining some post-visit contact, will help to turn them into committed ecotourists and ambassadors for conservation.

3. POINTS FOR FURTHER DEBATE

From the discussion and recommendations arising from the preparatory conferences, summarised above, it is possible to pull out some substantial issues in the area of product development and marketing for further debate at the World Ecotourism Summit.

• Strengthening the involvement of local and indigenous communities in product development, and the benefits they gain from it.

- Generating more conservation benefits from ecotourism product development and marketing.

- Helping protected areas support, and gain benefit from, the development and marketing of ecotourism products associated with them.

- Finding the best ways of linking together ecotourism products for mutual benefit, such as geographical clusters, associations of operators, vertical linkages between products and tour operators and transnational consortia.

- Understanding the breadth of the market for ecotourism products and its main components.

- Strengthening the delivery of technical and financial support for small ecotourism enterprises and community-based initiatives.

- Improving the exchange of know-how and good practice between projects.

- Encouraging national and local government and tourist organisations to do more to promote ecotourism and improve the conditions for its development and success in destinations.

- Strengthening the application of web-based marketing tools.

- Making sure that tourists are getting the right level of information, including what is expected of them as well as what they should expect.

- Raising the profile of ecotourism, and the principles it embodies, through a promotional campaign at an international level.

THEME D:
MONITORING THE COSTS AND BENEFITS OF ECOTOURISM:
EQUITABLE DISTRIBUTION BETWEEN ALL ACTORS

WTO/UNEP Summary of Preparatory Conferences
to serve as
Discussion Paper for the World Ecotourism Summit,

Prepared by Prof. François Vellas

Monitoring the costs and benefits of ecotourism is vital to the success of a tourism development strategy based on the equitable distribution of benefits between all actors. Such a strategy must be built on the will of the international, national and local public sector agencies to support a tourism development approach based on ecotourism principles as well as on strong (i.e. profitable) tourism firms for which ecotourism is not just a slogan but a means of ensuring the sustainability of their activities and of developing new opportunities for growth.

1. ISSUES DISCUSSED

Ecotourism encompasses all forms of tourism focused on nature where the principal motivation is to observe and appreciate nature and traditional cultures living in natural areas. Therefore, ecotourism is generally organized for small groups and involves an element of education and interpretation. It must provide positive impacts on the natural and socio-cultural environment, and any negative impacts must be limited and controlled.

Thus, the measurement of economic, ecological and social costs and benefits of ecotourism is different from that of traditional tourism. The ratios used in these measurements, particularly those evaluating economic profitability, must go beyond merely measuring financial profitability and take into account the impact on the local population's income, activities, and social conditions.

1.1 - Measuring economic costs and benefits of ecotourism

The measurement of the economic costs and benefits of traditional tourism is based on a ratio of estimated profitability of the tourism investment using a methodology of market surveys and of load factor/occupancy determination. Calculating the appropriate coefficient of occupancy determines the profitability of tourism investments. Therefore operators aim to achieve and exceed a breakeven occupancy to ensure return-on-investment and maximum profit.

The Gross Operating Result (GOR) is the basic indicator used to measure the economic costs and benefits of tourism investments. The decision to go ahead with a tourism project will be made by comparing the budget available for financing the investment and with the total amount of the investment without taking into account the environmental costs or the social impact of the project.

For ecotourism projects, this type of economic and financial analysis is not generally sufficient. The cost benefit analysis of ecotourism projects cannot be just calculated in terms of potential profitability but must also take into account costs and benefits for local populations.

The many examples of cost benefit analyses of ecotourism projects presented during various regional seminars show that even with an accommodation occupancy rate of only 20%, local population income increases substantially, and often provides more than double the income derived from agriculture.

Yet traditional financial analysis would indicate that such occupancy rates would be too low compared to the norm and therefore the investment would be abandoned. Based on the conclusions of these regional seminars, in particular those in the Seychelles, Mozambique and Belize, it is recommended that whilst profitability is vital the measurement of economic costs and benefits must be taken into account. The following factors must be considered:

in terms of economic costs as for instance:

- The cost of energy infrastructure (existence or lack of renewable energy sources)
- The cost of transport infrastructure and access to ecotourism sites (roads and access roads)
- The cost of providing drinkable water
- The cost of waste treatment (solid and sewage)

in terms of economic benefits, as for instance:

- Increased income benefits for the local populations
- Tax receipt benefits for the national public authorities
- Royalties and access right benefits for the local public authorities

1.2- Measuring ecological costs and benefits of ecotourism

The measurement of the ecological costs and benefits of tourism projects is a keystone of ecotourism development. Indeed, ecotourism development is one of the rare forms of tourism development, which under certain conditions can support the protection of the natural zones through conservation programmes that it may initiate and finance.

The instruments used to measure the ecological costs and benefits are mainly composite indicators to determine the pressure and intensity of use on ecotourism sites. The WTO defines three composite indicators particularly well adapted to measure ecological costs and benefits:

- **Carrying capacity**: this composite indicator determines the maximum number tourists that a site can hold, particularly during intensive use in peak period. This indicator can be calculated using indices of protection of the natural sites and indicates the capacity of the site to support different volumes of visitors.

- **Site stress**: this composite indicator measures impact levels on the site taking into account its natural and ecological characteristics. Despite all precautions taken to limit damage to the natural environment, ecotourism still produces some negative impacts, this indicator measures the extent of these negative impacts and signals when action must be taken to minimise these.

- **Attractiveness**: this measures the ecological characteristics of the site that are attractive for ecotourism and which may change over time and with increasing intensity of tourist visits. This is a qualitative indicator, which plays a very important part in ensuring the sustainability of ecotourism investments.

These indicators contribute to the efficient ecological monitoring of ecotourism products and provide an overall vision of the various products created in the same geographical area by all the different operators.

1.3 - The measurement of social costs and benefits of ecotourism

The measurement of social costs and benefits of ecotourism projects indicates the extent that ecotourism achieves one of its principal goals i.e. the equitable distribution of benefits between all the actors. The conclusions of the majority of the regional seminars on the subject, in particular those in Brazil, Kazakhstan and Maldives, clearly show that one of the main priorities of ecotourism is to provide local populations with economic and social benefits.

However, ecotourism may also have social costs, which are rarely taken into account. It is not just sufficient to measure the tourist/resident ratio; the degree of local population satisfaction must also be evaluated. The following indices are used to measure this:

in terms of social cost:

- Disturbance to the rate/rhythm of the local population's working lives (time of work related to tourism compared to normal schedules of work);

- Disturbance to the traditional use of space by the local population because of the routes used by the ecotourists;

- Disturbance of the local population's eating habits and everyday life as a result of contact with tourists

in terms of social benefits:

- Creation of employment and new activities related to ecotourism

- Improvement in comfort, living conditions and social services (electricity, access to healthcare and education, etc.)

- Measurement of the local population's degree of satisfaction through surveys.

These indicators provide the tools to evaluate the potential and real impacts of ecotourism and its contribution to nature conservation.

1.4 - The contribution to nature conservation and evaluation of the impact of ecotourism on the environment, society and culture

Ecotourism contributes to nature conservation by providing economic benefits to host communities, and organizations and administrations in charge of environmental protection and natural areas. As such, ecotourism not only creates jobs and provides local populations with sources of income, but it also creates awareness amongst both inhabitants and tourists of the need to preserve the natural and cultural capital.

As frequently emphasised by participants at regional conferences the assessment of potential and real impacts of ecotourism on the environment, society and culture and the need for evaluation tools are vital. Thus, the Tourism Satellite Account (TSA) model could be adapted to measure the impact of the ecotourism on the environment and society.

The TSA implementation project published by the WTO in 2001 states clearly that the conceptual framework of the TSA can be widened to integrate a sectoral and spatial focus to include environmental and social costs of tourism as well as economic benefits. Therefore, the TSA could become the most appropriate tool to measure the impact of tourism, in particular:

- the cost of employment lost in agriculture caused by the increase in tourism activity
- the damage caused to the ecosystem
- the damage to biodiversity
- goods and services which become too expensive for the local population because of inflation as a result of demand by tourists and their suppliers

TSA are based on Input/Output tables (I/O) which show the relationship between different sectors and activities of production and how benefits are used and redistributed. The impact of ecotourism could be compared with that of other forms of tourism development using TSA I/O tables.

However, because of the qualitative aspects linked to culture, the impact of ecotourism on culture requires specific analysis. Thus a case-by-case approach must be adopted.

Tourism activities in rural communities should be conceived as complementary to traditional economic activities. This needs to be so for two main reasons: firstly, to multiply the linkages of ecotourism with other, traditional economic activities, such as agriculture, fishing, handicrafts and others; and secondly, to avoid overdependence of the local economy and jobs on tourism alone.

2. RECOMMENDATIONS

Adopting precautionary measures at the local, national, regional and international levels: The objective of precautionary measures is not to discourage the development of ecotourism, but to ensure efficient coordination between the local, national, regional and international levels in order to guarantee the sustainability of ecotourism sites. However, as reported in discussions during the regional seminars, in particular those in the Seychelles, Algeria and Greece, the total cost of the environmental protection of ecotourism destinations may exceed the financial benefits.

In this case applying the principle of the "polluter pays" and the principle of the "user pays" may not guarantee that all the costs of environmental protection will be covered and it is the responsibility of the public authorities to make up the rest. Five types of measures may be considered:

- **Increasing the resistance of sites**. With international assistance, national and local authorities in charge of the environmental protection of natural sites can artificially increase their resistance by protecting them with barriers and routings that prevent direct visitor access to in the most sensitive zones where conservation problems may occur, as is the case in small islands.

- **Varying ecotourism activity in time and space** so that visitors are not always directed towards the same places at the same time, for example in arid and desert regions. This requires precise coordination between local and national authorities.

- **Strictly reducing the number of visitors admitted to certain sites**, in particular mountain sites, even (and especially) in high tourist season. This measure can cause conflicts between international, regional, national and especially local partners because of the economic stakes involved.

- **Regulating the amount of time allowed for visits to the sites as well as schedules** according to the frequency of visitation and the period of the year, in particular in certain islands of the Mediterranean, which receive a large number of ecotourists.

- **Restricting access according to tourists groups and their sensitivity toward the protection of sites**. This measure can be implemented by imposing guides with competencies specific to the sites visited. It also requires tight coordination between national and local authorities, particularly in the case of wildlife conservation parks in Africa, as mentioned during the seminar organized in Mozambique.

3. CONCRETE PROPOSALS

Integrating monitoring and evaluation methods: concrete proposals

Evaluation methodology must be based on the constant monitoring of ecotourism activities in order to ensure that they are meeting the required objectives. This entails the use of environmental, social and economic evaluation indicators as the most appropriate tools for monitoring.

3.1 – Integrating monitoring

A selection of indicators that can be used to evaluate projects and ecotourism activities include:

- Local resident per capita budget allocated by government to nature conservation and the management of the environment
- The surface area of protected zones expressed as a percentage of the country's or area surface area in which ecotourism projects are developed.
- The number of rare species in the ecosystems of ecotourism destination
- Number of tourists in proportion to the number of residents
- Number of tourists by surface area of the protected zone
- Trend in number of firms in the area over time
- Number of tourist firms using an ecolabel
- Impact on local production indicator
- Development control indicator
- Mechanisms to reinvest ecotourism receipts for site protection

3.2 – Evaluation methods

Selecting the appropriate indicators to be used in the evaluation and monitoring of ecotourism projects can be problematic. Indeed, for greater effectiveness, it is advisable to determine distinct quantitative evaluation criteria or at least a range as standards for each type of tourism or area. These standards for the selected indicators must be elaborated in co-operation with the national and local authorities responsible for tourism so that they become operational in each country and in each area.

- Quantitative and qualitative liquid and solid waste processing indicators with a system adapted to process waste produced by tourists
- Cultural impact indicator
- Training indicator
- Job creation indicator
- Water and energy consumption indicators (use of renewable energy)
- Indicator of visits by the local population
- New technology usage indicator

These can be used as references by the authorities in charge of tourism development and are an effective method to check whether the objectives of sustainable tourism planning are being met by private tourism development projects and whether these projects should be encouraged to be continued or held back.

The proposed ratios for the evaluation indicators must be balanced according to their perceived importance for each area or tourist zone. Furthermore, it has been suggested at the regional conferences and seminars that monitoring itself is not sufficient without responsive measures and management actions, and that it must be accompanied by mechanisms to recover the capital invested in ecotourism projects to benefit ecological projects and nature conservation, so that the development of ecotourism is truly compatible with better protection of natural zones.

3.3 - The need for studies and evolutionary management systems

To ensure accurate monitoring of the costs and benefits of ecotourism, an equitable distribution of these benefits and to guarantee long-term success a management system based on public/private sector partnership is vital. Evolutionary, management systems for ecotourism are based on an institutional framework comprising long-term policies to facilitate the development of tourism investments. This framework should include a consultation mechanism with operators and the local population to review the design and implementation of ecotourism projects. Local people should participate more as entrepreneurs and decision-makers in tourism and not only as employees as now is often the case. Small scale, locally owned tourism is considered the most appropriate means to achieve this given that benefits could flow directly to the local populations. This often requires appropriate support and mentoring together with training opportunities.

The framework should also comprise a strict control system for tourism investments to ensure that the projects that are developed respect environmental protection criteria for the area.

From the discussion and recommendations arising from Theme D of the preparatory meetings and regional conferences, the main issues related to monitoring ecotourism's costs and benefits and to ensuring an equitable distribution among all stakeholders can be highlighted.

4. POINTS FOR FURTHER DEBATE

The following issues could be discussed at the World Tourism Summit:

• Devising new ecotourism cost/benefit evaluation methods which would highlight the social and economic benefits for local populations, as well as the limitations of the financial benefits generated compared to other forms of tourism, notably mass tourism.

- Finding appropriate legal and institutional mechanisms to facilitate and make effective the systematic participation of local communities in the overall ecotourism process, including policy definition, planning, management and monitoring.

- Establishing financial and fiscal mechanisms to ensure that a significant proportion of the income generated from ecotourism remains with the local community or serves conservation purposes.

- Researching methods to ensure the permanent control of impacts through the adaptation of carrying capacity methodologies to ecotourism development, including the definition of damage warning indicators and disturbance gauges for protected sites and other natural areas.

- Putting in place distribution mechanisms to share the benefits of ecotourism development in order to reinvest a proportion of the revenues generated in the protected areas.

- Understanding and measuring social costs, benefits and change (i.e. changes in the behaviour and habits of the local population) so as to limit the negative consequences, maximising social benefits for host communities and to improve attitudes, awareness and respect towards the protection of the environment.

- Researching specific management and monitoring procedures for different types of ecotourism sites, (i.e. desert zones and islands), concerning such aspects as water and waste management, the management of scarce resources, and others.

- Determining appropriate price levels to ensure sufficient returns for firms, suitable redistribution in favour of local populations and that correspond to the purchasing power of tourism demand.

- Ensuring that the principles of "polluter pays" and "user pays" will ensure genuine protection of the environment whilst guaranteeing ecotourism development.

ANNEX 2

SUSTAINABLE DEVELOPMENT OF ECOTOURISM WEB CONFERENCE

Preparatory Conference for the International Year of Ecotourism April 1-26, 2002

FINAL REPORT

INTRODUCTION

Over the past two decades ecotourism activities have expanded rapidly and further growth is expected in the future. Recognizing its global importance, the United Nations designated the year 2002 as the International Year of Ecotourism, and its Commission on Sustainable Development requested international agencies, governments and the private sector to undertake supportive activities.

In this framework the World Tourism Organization (WTO) and the United Nations Environment Programme (UNEP) organized a pioneering forum that was conducted solely online the Internet. The Conference was developed and moderated by Ron Mader, author and webhost of the Planeta.com website.

The prime objective of the conference was to provide easy access for a wide range of stakeholders involved in ecotourism to exchange experiences and voice comments, especially for those who had not been able to attend the regional preparatory conferences that had taken place in the past year.

The experience and results derived from the Sustainable Development of Ecotourism Web Conference will be presented at the World Ecotourism Summit in Quebec, Canada (19-22 May 2002).

More than 900 stakeholders from 97 countries participated in this Conference, representing international, public and private organizations, NGOs, academic institutions and local communities. During the event, more than 100 messages, received from around 30 countries, were posted and archived for future reference. Participants shared information through case studies, specific examples and field experiences, and recommended resources for those interested in ecotourism issues. Intensive debates developed on some messages, analyzing specific topics from a range of views. Archives can be freely consulted online
>> **http://groups.yahoo.com/group2002ecotourism**

Participants were asked to send messages in English, Spanish and French.

The discussion was focused on four main themes defined for the World Ecotourism Summit, in four thematic sessions addressed in each of the four weeks of the event:

- Theme 1:   Ecotourism Policy and Planning: The Sustainability Challenge
- Theme 2:   Regulation of Ecotourism: Institutional Responsibilities and Frameworks
- Theme 3:   Product Development, Marketing and Promotion of Ecotourism: Fostering Sustainable Products and Consumers
- Theme 4:   Monitoring Costs and Benefits of Ecotourism: Ensuring Equitable Distribution among all Stakeholders

As in other preparatory conferences for the World Ecotourism Summit, there was some overlap in the dialogue, particularly at the beginning of each theme week. Participants often consciously chose to mix their responses to various topics in a single post. These messages provided particularly useful insights to the complex nature of the ecotourism market.

A draft of this summary report was circulated among participants for comments.

SUMMARY OF DISCUSSIONS

Throughout the four-week conference there was a thoughtful dialogue about the complexities of ecotourism. Several participants indicated that the process leading up to the World Ecotourism Summit and the Summit itself present a major opportunity to promote mutually reinforcing relationships that exist among tourism operations, conservation, and local community development.

As ecotourism has dramatically captured the attention of people around the world, there are many expectations of what ecotourism can offer for a particular locality, as well for larger regions and in the global environmental movement.

There was a plethora of discussion about definitions that should be used in this field. There was also a healthy dialogue about the type of ecotourism that can and should be promoted. Discussions drew from the complexities of ecotourism regulation, certification, product development and marketing. Of note were repeated comments and dialogue about positive and negative impacts of tourism on communities and local people.

There is a growing concern that ecotourism is such a powerful force driven by the world's largest industry and participants stressed that it is essential that the ecotourism sector remains a low impact niche.

Several participants questioned whether travel could be considered a sustainable activity, because of basic environmental impacts associated with the use of motor vehicles and aircrafts. These questions led participants into a productive dialogue about available information resources as well as the need for continued study and the development of action plans.

THEME 1:
Ecotourism Policy and Planning: The Sustainability Challenge

Questions: Participants were asked to reflect on how effective are ecotourism plans at the international, national and local levels in promoting sustainable ecotourism. Among other questions, they were asked whether ecotourism policies integrate with wider planning frameworks and what is the most efficient way to balance conservation and development objectives in ecotourism policies.

Overview: Participants presented edited case studies of ecotourism policy from Brazil, Chile, Cuba, Ecuador, Hungary, India, Malaysia, Pakistan and Venezuela. Of special note were discussions that linked successful management of protected areas to the inclusion of local people and stakeholders.

Comments and Conclusions

- The conceptual and practical workings of ecotourism have been isolated from each other too long. Ecotourism development should focus on action plans and not become, as one participant complained, "bogged down" in definitions.

- Ecotourism promoted by single organizations with single objectives, without involving all stakeholder groups affected, lead to poorly balanced strategies. Governments, environmental and social groups, the private sector, academics and local communities need to work jointly towards the development of effective ecotourism policies.

- The governments' role in ecotourism development is to provide the overall policy environment to permit development to proceed along an orderly path. This framework needs to clearly involve and welcome participation of other sectors. Ecotourism plans should be widely circulated among community members, NGOs, government agencies, travel companies and other stakeholders.

- There has been a lag in governmental response to development that threatens conservation of protected areas at many destinations. Obstacles include a lack of qualified personnel, lack of continuity and lack of interest in small scale ecotourism operations.

- Policy making lies often in the hands of people with limited field business experience. This leads to regulations that are not feasible at the ground level and consequently are not implemented. Said one participant: "The cycle of impossible laws, blatant non-compliance, corruption and disbelief in the legal system is a constraint for businesses aiming at ecotourism operations in a sustainable way. Therefore, policy is often incongruous with reality." When policy makers do not have the background in this field or experience in the local area, there is a need to teach policy makers so that policies reflect social and environmental concerns as well as market realities.

- National directives are often unimplemented because of lack of cross sector commitment from various ministries or lack of continuity. High turn-over and poor communication between government offices were cited as chief causes of this problem.

- While national level policies are important to ecotourism, development takes place at the local level. Local authorities play a key role, and in many localities a bottom-up approach to ecotourism planning is desirable. There is a great need for cooperation between authorities at different levels. Also, legal standards need to be integrated so that the structure supports the development of ecotourism.

- Development plans need to identify financial sources and financing mechanisms for local, regional and national programs and cultivate these resources for long-term investment. Ecotourism projects rarely succeed as quickly or as profitably as other sectors, so ecotourism requires long-term financial commitment.

- Ecotourism operations may cause a negative impact on local populations. Tourism can drive up local prices and force locals to move away or restrictive policies lead businesses to develop operations elsewhere. Ecotourism for protected areas must bring indirect conflict resolution with local people/stakeholders, education for visitors; financial income from tourism for communities living within or adjacent to those areas.

- It is to everyone's advantage that nature based tourism operations move increasingly towards adoption of the principles of ecotourism, to ensure that sensitive natural areas are conserved and local community and cultural benefits are maximized.

THEME 2:
Regulation of Ecotourism:
Institutional Responsibilities and Frameworks

Questions: Participants were asked to reflect on how policies and plans can be implemented and what are the positive and negative effects of these regulations on stakeholders and on the environment of ecotourism sites? Among other issues, they were asked about what the role is and could be of ecotourism certification and who benefits from such programs.

Overview: Participants provided numerous examples about regulation, including detailed essays about tourism certification in Brazil, tourism legislation in Venezuela and community tourism in Ecuador. Others noted the absence of legal mechanisms ensuring repayment of economic activity income to the protected area. Participants also brought up the pros and cons of certification programs.

Comments and Conclusions

- If regulation is too strict it can hamper competitiveness, and operators or countries can be placed at a disadvantage. On the other hand, if consumers place an economic value on healthy ecosystems, the market will drive all operators to achieve higher levels of environmental stewardship.

- Regulation will not work effectively if the community, the tour operator, tour guide and tourists themselves do not share the same concept of ecotourism. The concepts must be relevant to all stakeholders. Successful ecotourism development requires agreements on definitions and consistent legislation.

- Effective certification programs need to inform the traveling public about ecotourism products and services. Certification and accreditation should include as a priority a campaign and a coalition of media and communication professionals that effectively deliver the message. If clients are not requesting certification standards, one participant argued the practice may be "putting the cart before the horse."

- Other participants noted that even if certification schemes are not sought by tourism consumers, business-to-business operations do pursue them. Well designed certification programs can help achieve the objectives of ecotourism by providing incentives to certified ecotourism operators with a marketing advantage.

- National broad-based coalitions have the best records for developing certification. One example frequently cited is Australia's National Ecotourism Accreditation Programme (NEAP) which has developed as the result of multi-sector discussions among the government, private sector and academics.

THEME 3:
Product Development, Marketing and Promotion of Ecotourism: Fostering Sustainable Products and Consumers

Questions: Participants were asked to reflect on challenges and opportunities of ecotourism product development and marketing. Among other questions, Participants were asked what role is played by public and private protected area managers and the private sector. Also, what marketing and promotional techniques have proven to be effective and how participants saw the role of transnational corporations, hotel chains and franchises in facilitating sustainable tourism development and supporting local tourism businesses.

Overview: Participants recounted examples about product development and marketing in Argentina, Brazil, Canada, China, Chile, Ecuador, France, Spain, the United Kingdom, and the United States.

A lively discussion over competing versions of ecotourism that needed to be promoted emerged during the third week. As one participant commented: "Like the environmental movement, there is room in ecotourism for many different styles. Just as a road protester chaining himself to a tree and a lawyer in a three-piece suit may be fighting for the same thing, and they are both necessary and worthwhile, ecotourism needs both the high-end, no microphones, one-at-a-time operator and the more mainstream, wholesale crowd pleaser."

Not surprising for a conference conducted online, participants discussed the role of Internet in ecotourism development, particularly in marketing and promotion. Participants agreed that, particularly in this niche market of ecotourism and responsible travel, websites play an important role in developing consumer awareness and environmental education. Several website directors explained their operations. Of note were suggestions of how travelers could review the tour operators on the web, enforcing the standards of the operators. Other sites encourage a regional dialogue among stakeholders. Participants also noted that improved access and training will be necessary to "bridge the digital divide" as many parts of the world are less wired than others.

Comments and Conclusions

- Educating consumers is key to raising awareness and stimulating demand for socially- and environmentally-friendly products and services. The hardest sale to make is to the first-time ecotourist. As one participants argued: "Once people have a chance to stay in an ecolodge and to use guided services, they are likely to become loyal customers."

- The stimulation for ecologically sensitive products should be the key driver to improving ecotourism. One participant said, "This should be done through customer education rather than through regulation."

- Media coverage does not adequately address the substance of ecotourism. One example: nature shows often focuses on dangerous animals or scenic landscapes and leave out the human part of the equation.

- Information needs to be accurate. For example, if a sign reads that a path is 1 kilometer when in reality it is two or if at the end of a hike the expected meal or refreshment is not ready, the reputation of the tour is damaged by not meeting the expectations of the traveler. If the service does not meet expectations, the situation has the potential to harm the reputation of all regional operations.

- The principal aim of an ecotourism business should be achieving high levels of satisfaction among its clients by providing quality services and contributing to the conservation of the natural and cultural resources.

- Initiatives to develop and promote ecotourism are frequently divided among private sector and government programs. In Ecuador, for example, the past three years have seen stronger cooperation and improved results.

Internet Use

- The Internet is a highly efficient, cheap and ecological way for communities to reach and be reached by ecotourists directly. The challenge lies in bridging the digital divide and providing the training required by communities to master this medium. Patience and continuity are key ingredients for success. If such training is not provided, the Internet will not fulfill its promise of leveling the small vs. large operator promotional playing field.

- The experience of ecotourism operations that have successfully promoted their products and services online show that the Internet is a powerful tool for even the smallest operations. Regular access has been shown to help communities communicate and share information.

- Government tourism offices, environmental groups and companies need to improve their use of the Web as soon as possible.

- The increasing use of Internet by ecotourists was demonstrated, for example, through the Rural Ecotourism Assessment Project in Belize where tourists were asked what types of marketing they had encountered pre-trip, and more than two thirds said they had encountered web sites, second only to word of mouth.

- There is an untapped potential in Internet cafes in tourist centers. One participant suggested that cybercafe computers could "have a start page directing travelers to information on local sites or to a central consumer-oriented site."

Product Development

- Most comments underlined the inherent need for ecotourism marketing in development projects and operations, as a basic component for economic sustainability. One participant warned: "Noble, well-intentioned ecotourism programs fail if the heralded ecotourists do not arrive."

- Because the definition of ecotourism is vague, ecotourism developers and consumers are challenged by what the marketing message should be.

- A good marketing plan should include a well-balanced, multi-media approach. Use of the Web should be complimented with traditional marketing.

- Ecotourism operations need educated, empowered and inspired travelers. For this tour operators and service providers should inform and educate consumers they depart for a trip, or even before they make decision and book for a trip.

- Tourists don't want to be just "educated." As one participant stated: "They want to have a safe, interesting vacation, worth their money and time".

- The tourism market is complex and there is no static profile of the "ecotourist".

117

- The results of investigations, and assessments of the "ecotourism market" are widely divergent, as survey methods and sources of information are varied. WTO researched existing market data as part of its Ecotourism Market Study Series, conducted in the 7 major ecotourism generating countries of Europe and North America. For example, the 1994 Ecotourism-Nature/Adventure/Culture: Alberta and British Columbia (Canada) Market Demand Assessment suggested that there was an ecotourism market of 13.2 million travelers (representing 77% of all respondents) in just seven of the major urban areas in North America. The ecotourism definition used was "tourism related to nature/adventure/culture in the countryside". An In-Flight Survey on US travelers to overseas and Mexico, conducted by the US Department of Commerce in 1996 and 1999 suggests that the market represents 4% of US international travelers, and they spend less on average than the typical US traveler. This survey used the qualification that the ecotourists had to have participated in environmental or ecological excursions. In conclusion, it is necessary to further improve and coordinate ecotourism market research activities to provide more complete data on market trends. WTO applied a coordinated research methodology for its Ecotourism Market Study Series that implied surveys with specialized tour operators and tourists, in addition to the analysis of existing market data, in each country markets.

- Developing a product requires understanding client needs and a level of education and marketing that promotes the products and services in the niche of ecotourism. Marketing, however, is never as simple as "build it and they will come." Many planners working in product development don't have a clear idea of market competition. Citing work in the Amazon, one participant questioned the efficiency of a community-prepared brochure: "People have the idea that if they have a nice waterfall, it alone is worth the time for foreigners to visit."

- Air travel is the fastest growing source of greenhouse gas emissions in the world. According to one participant, "on an eight hour flight, each passenger is responsible for releasing the equivalent of one ton of carbon dioxide into the atmosphere. If ecotourism is to be sustainable, it needs to address the aviation issue and give travelers the option of doing something to repair the damage they do." Other participants added that the entire scope of transportation needs to be evaluated.

THEME 4:
Monitoring Costs and Benefits of Ecotourism: Ensuring Equitable Distribution among all Stakeholders

Questions: Participants were asked to reflect on how the principles of ecotourism could be measured and monitored. Among other questions, they were asked for field experience and ideas on how local steward communities, park personnel, tourists and tour operators participate in monitoring activities.

Overview: Case studies of monitoring costs and benefits were provided from Argentina, Brazil, Bulgaria, Ecuador, Georgia, Hungary, Iceland, India, Mexico, Romania, Russia, South Africa, Turkey and Ukraine.

Comments and Conclusions

- Because the definition of ecotourism is vague, ecotourism developers and consumers are challenged by what the marketing message should be.

- It is necessary to have widely accepted terms of a definition for ecotourism and some consistent standards for the proper evaluation of the costs and benefits of ecotourism.

- It's difficult to imagine effective cost/benefit analysis without developing adequate baseline data, research mechanisms, or improving basic information sharing as quickly as possible. Those developing or investing in ecotourism need to share information about the successes and failures of projects integrating nature tourism and conservation.

- The costs and benefits of ecotourism are often social, so these factors need to be included in a holistic monitoring program. "There is no easy model to evaluate all the true costs and benefits beyond the financial value," said one participant, adding that the full payoff may be many years down the road.

- While talking about indicators, it is clear that they must be developed by all the project's stakeholders. In terms of the environment and local cultures, ecotourism destinations tend to be fragile areas. Consequently, contacts must bridge environmental and tourism interests. Examples were given from case studies at Lake Balaton, Hungary and the Valdes Peninsula, Argentina, from workshops and pilot projects conducted by WTO on sustainable tourism indicators. WTO has established a task force to prepare a new manual on the identification and application of sustainability indicators in tourism development.

- Governments need to implement a system of monitoring in potential development areas and have a comprehensive action plan to respond to a development boom in ecologically sensitive areas and the surrounding communities. Satellite accounting, being developed under the coordination of World Tourism Organization offers a number of benefits to measure the impacts of ecotourism.

- Many developing countries are particularly weak in providing access to timely information about current developments, investment opportunities, guidelines and best case examples. These resources need to be available for all stakeholders and written in a language directed toward their target audience.

- There are both positive and negative implications for local ecotourism businesses working with transnationals. Local ecotourism business could benefit from partnerships with transnationals and bigger companies.The role of the transnational tourism company or hotel chain can be one of partner, competitor or investor. The ecotourism operator has some power over how the big companies will operate. One participant advised that "the operator must learn to think like a transnational" in order to work with them. Another participant said that "transnational does not necessarily mean enormous nor inhumane."

Information-Sharing Proposals:

The Center for Sustainable Tourism at the University of Colorado announced that is developing an online data bank, in collaboration with UNEP and WTO, focusing on ecotourism/sustainable tourism. It will contain a broad range of documents developed in the framework of the International Year of Ecotourism by a wide range of organizations.

Planeta.com suggested developing a working group that could develop an initiative that would promote the most effective means of communication among stakeholders. Each would be responsible for updating their website with a minimum amount of information.

SPOTLIGHT ON COMMUNITY TOURISM

As a cross-cutting issue, community tourism was addressed throughout the conference. Some participants argued that ecotourism must stress the "maximum participation of local people" -- others questioned who could be considered a local.

Comments and Conclusions

- Communities that obtain income from ecotourism develop environmental awareness about their own unique ecosystems. In a study funded by the International Labour Organization in Ecuador, Peru and Bolivia, a participant noted that the ecotourism activity has reinforced a process of ethnic awareness. Ecuador has pursued this study with the creation of a database of all community-based tourism operations.

- Community-based ecotourism requires political organization. Said one participant: "The emergence of community-based ecotourism projects is directly linked to the political organization of indigenous and social movements. These projects offer an alternative to fight against poverty, injustice, discrimination and environmental destruction." Successful community-based ecotourism requires a level of specialization that goes beyond "good intentions." Another participant commented about working with communities on ecotourism: "It's not enough to have specialization in biology or anthropology, the process is long and requires a better understanding of the tourism market and community dynamics."

- Obstacles to community-based ecotourism often include the lack of a legal framework, promotion and marketing and interference from traditional industries that can destroy the local environment.

- Communities that live in the areas of high biodiversity where community-based ecotourism could be successful often do not have the financial resources to get the training and supplies, infrastructure and vehicles to be successful.

- Multinational development projects often exclude local peoples. For example, one participant pointed out that in the development of Mesoamerica's Plan Puebla Panama, ecotourism development favors large hotel corporations and not the indigenous federations or small scale initiatives.

- Unregulated community tourism may pose environmental harm while providing social benefits. Said one participant: "I've seen a dolphin-watching operation in north Bali, where the local community have democratically worked out a system for sharing the economic benefits: no one can have more than four people on their boat, so everyone gets to work. The result is 50 boats and one pod of dolphins. The best thing that could happen for these dolphins is for a multinational company to come along, put one or two big boats in the water, employ all the locals and to do marketing. There may be some unemployed, some of the profits might go elsewhere, but the dolphins would be a lot safer."

- Some local ecotourism ventures might complain that working with tour operators and travel agents means sharing revenues with "outsiders.", but as a participant stated: "As in other commercial sectors there are middle men who bring buyers and sellers together. This is a legitimate value-added service."

- For aboriginal or indigenous communities, ecotourism represents a development opportunity that can bring many economic, environmental, cultural, social and political benefits. Said one participant: "The key for Indigenous communities to achieve these benefits is active involvement in, and genuine control over, ecotourism initiatives within their traditional territory. To achieve involvement and control, Indigenous communities must be much more than token players receiving fringe employment or craft sales benefits."

- Active involvement and control of ecotourism products and services by Indigenous communities will not only benefit Indigenous peoples. One participant wrote: "A vibrant and successful Indigenous ecotourism sector will greatly strengthen ecotourism as a global industry. The richness and diversity of Indigenous cultures and traditional knowledge is an incredible resource for the ecotourism industry."

RECOMMENDATIONS

The following are general recommendations that emerged during the Sustainable Development of Ecotourism Web Conference:

- Ecotourism should balance top-down and bottom-up development strategies.

- Effective standards are the result of a consensus building process among all affected interests.

- Policy makers need to learn more about ecotourism as practiced in the field, not only as designed in the office or classroom.

- National development policies need to be harmonized to favor ecotourism planning; at the very least, national policies should not undermine ecotourism development.

- Priority should be given in the training of local people and park managers and to monitoring the delivery of services and products to insure they meet expectations.

- An umbrella organization of multi-sector ecotourism enterprises and public authorities should be created to develop and market a particular region. Membership in this organization should not be priced out of the reach of small local operators.

- Accessible financing (grants, inexpensive long-term loans) is needed for ecotourism projects and must include ways to measure whether these monies are being used effectively.

- Internet communication provides a low-cost and efficient mechanism for both promotion and development; it needs to be complimented with other communication strategies.

- Information needs to be accurate; access to timely and useful information needs to be improved for all stakeholders.

- Media professionals need to provide better insights into ecotourism without losing the human dimension.

REFERENCES

• SUSTAINABLE DEVELOPMENT OF ECOTOURISM CONFERENCE ARCHIVE
>> http://groups.yahoo.com/group/2002ecotourism
- This archive is automatically updated throughout the event and may be searched and accessed by the public.

• PLANETA.COM
>> http://www.planeta.com/2002ecotourism.html
- This conference center page provides a short synthesis of the aims and deadlines of the conference. It also provides links to an index of messages posted during the event and the list of questions we asked participants to answer. The center also includes tips on online conferencing and troubleshooting assistance.

Another key document is the IYE 2002 Resource Guide
>> http://www.planeta.com/ecotravel/tour/year.html
- This document provides links to official events, summaries, criticism and related initiatives to the International Year of Ecotourism. The page is regularly updated with corrections and suggestions made in the ongoing IYE2002 Forum <http://groups.yahoo.com/group/iye2002>.

• UNITED NATIONS ENVIRONMENT PROGRAMME
>> http://www.uneptie.org/pc/tourism/ecotourism/documents.htm
- This site provides the information about UNEP ecotourism studies, including backgrounders on the IYE objectives, and UNEP's partners and activities. The site links to summary reports from preparatory conferences and includes a number of documents in PDF format.

• WORLD TOURISM ORGANIZATION
>> http://www.world-tourism.org/sustainable/IYE-Main-Menu.htm
- This website includes updated news on international, regional and national activities in the framework of the International year of Ecotourism 2002 and related activities, including links to final reports from various preparatory conferences, and press releases, as well as information about WTO publications. Its page <http://www.world-tourism.org/2002ecotourism> served for basic information, background documents and registration for the Sustainable Development of Ecotourism Web Conference. In addition to this information, this page now contains the complete final report and an evaluation of the web-conference.

ANNEX 3

Final Programme of the World Ecotourism Summit

Québec City, Canada

Programme

Sunday 19 May 2002

5.00 p.m. – 6.00 p.m.   Opening Ceremony

- Mr. Francesco Frangialli, Secretary-General, World Tourism Organization
- Mr. Klaus Töpfer, Executive Director, United Nations Environment Programme
- Mr. Judd Buchanan, President, Canadian Tourism Commission
- Mr. Richard Legendre, Minister of Tourism, Québec
- Mr. Jean-Paul Allier, Mayor of Québec City

6.00 p.m. – 7.00 p.m.   Cocktails and opening of the "Eco Rendez-vous"

7.00 p.m. – 10.00 p.m.   Reception Diner

Monday, 20 May

8.00 a.m. – 8.45 a.m.	Introductory presentations:

• Dr. Klaus Töpfer, Executive Director, United Nations
Environment Programme
• Mr. Francesco Frangialli, Secretary-General, World Tourism
Organization
• Mrs Francine Cousteau, The Cousteau Society

8.45 a.m. – 9.35 a.m.   Panel to report on regional preparatory meetings held in **Africa**

Moderator: Ms. Omotayo Omotosho, Nigeria

• Mr. Fernando Sumbana Junior, Minister of Tourism,
Mozambique
*WTO Seminar on Planning, Development and Management of
Ecotourism in Africa - Maputo, Mozambique, March 2001*

• Mrs Simone de Comarmond, Minister for Tourism and
Transport, Seychelles
*WTO/UNEP Conference on Sustainable Development and
Management of Ecotourism in Small Island Developing States
(SIDS) and other Small Islands - Mahé, Seychelles, December
2001*

• Mr. Hocine Labreche, Ministry of Tourism and Handicraft,
Algeria
WTO Seminar on Sustainable Development of Ecotourism in
Desert Areas - Algiers (Algeria), January 2002

• Mr. Ted Kombo, Mr. Tom Ole Sikar and Mr. Sheba Hanyurwa
UNEP/TIES Conference for East Africa, Nairobi, Kenya, March
2002

9.35 a.m. – 10.15 a.m.   Debate and summary

10.15 a.m. - 10.45 a.m.   Coffee break

10.45 a.m. – 11.45 a.m.   Panel to report on regional preparatory meetings held in **Asia
                           and the Pacific**

Moderator: Mr. Sapta Nirwandar, Indonesia

• Mr. Adama Bah Bah, Tourism Concern Gambia, and Tan Chi
Kiong, Ecumenical Coalition for Third World Tourism
*UNEP/ETE International NGO Workshop Tourism Towards
2002, New Delhi, India, September 2001*

• Mr. Babu Varghese and Mr. Rajiv Bhartari
*UNEP/TIES Conference for South Asia, Gangtok, India,
January 2002*

• Mr. Hassan Sobir, Minister of Tourism, Maldives
WTO *Asia-Pacific Ministerial Conference on Sustainable Development of Ecotourism - Maldives, February 2002*

• Mr. Khamlay Sipaseuth and Mrs Maria Monina Flores
UNEP/TIES Conference for Southeast Asia, Chiang Mai, Thailand, March 2002

• Mr. Amena Yauvoli, 1st. Secretary, Fiji Mission to the UN and Mr. Manoa Malani, Principal Tourism Officer, Ministry of Tourism, Fiji
WTO/APO Conference on Sustainable Development of Ecotourism in the South Pacific Islands - Fiji, April 2002

11.45 a.m. – 12.30 p.m.	Debate and summary
12.30 p.m. – 2.00 p.m.	Lunch
2.00 p.m. – 3.00 p.m.	Panel to report on regional preparatory meetings held in the **Americas**

Moderator: Mr. Hector Ceballos Lascurain, Mexico

• Mr. Luis Otavio Paiva, Vice-minister, Ministry of Tourism and Sport, President EMBRATUR, Brazil
WTO *Conference on Sustainable Development and Management of Ecotourism in the Americas - Cuiabá, Brazil, August 2001*

• Mrs Leyla Solano and Mr. Raúl Arias de Parra
UNEP/TIES Conference for Mesoamerica, Belize City, Belize, November 2001

• Mrs Martha Llano and Mr José Flores Velasco
UNEP/TIES Conference for Andean South America, Lima, Peru, February 2002

• Mr. Crescencio Resendiz-Hernández
*Oaxaca Declaration on Indigenous Tourism
Oaxaca, Mexico, March 2002*

• Mr. Ron Mader, journalist and editor/publisher
*UNEP/WTO Sustainable Development of Ecotourism Web Conference
(http://groups.yahoo.com/group/2002ecotourism/) April 2002*

• Mr. Oscar Iriani, Advisor of the Secretary of Tourism and Sport, Argentina
Conclusions of the First National Conference on Ecotourism, Buenos Aires, Argentina, April 2002

3.00 p.m. – 3.45 p.m.	Debate and summary

3.45 p.m. – 4.15 p.m.   Coffee break

4.15 p.m. – 5.15 p.m.   Panel to report on regional preparatory meetings held in **Europe**

Moderator: Ms. Sylvie Blangy, France

• Mr. Jan Kickert, Minister Counsellor at the Austrian Embassy in Canada
WTO/UNEP Conference on Ecotourism in Mountain Areas: A Challenge to Sustainable Development - St. Johann / Pongau and Werfenweng, Salzburg, Austria, September 2001

• Mr. Yevgeniy Nikitinskiy, Agency for Tourism and Sport, Kazakhstan
WTO Seminar on Ecotourism - Almaty, Kazakhstan, October 2001

• Mr. Michail Modinos, President, National Centre for Environment and Sustainable Tourism, Greece
WTO Conference on the development of Ecotourism: The International Experience and the Case of Greece - Thessaloniki, Greece, November 2001

• Mrs Sarah Leonard and Mrs Ann-Kristine Vinka
TIES Conference on Arctic Countries, Hemavan, Sweden, April 2002

• Mr. Mustafa Tasar, Minister of Tourism, Turkey
Ecotourism in Turkey

5.15 p.m. – 6.00 p.m.   Debate and summary

6.00 p.m. – 6.30 p.m.   Free time

6.30 p.m. – 7.15 p.m.   Shuttle to the "Vieux Port"

7.30 p.m. – 10.30 p.m.   Dinner

Tuesday, 21 May

Four sessions in parallel:

Theme A: Ecotourism policies and planning

8.30 a.m. –9.45 a.m.	Welcome by Moderator Mr. Andreu Raya, Andorra

Introduction by Ms. Pamela Wight, WTO/UNEP expert

Mrs. Ellen Bertrand, Director, Parks Canada
Ecotourism Planning in Canadian Parks

Ms. Marie Lequin, Université du Québec à Trois-Rivières
Ecotourism and Participative Governance

Statements:

Mr. Gaylard Kombanwi, Permanent Secretary, Ministry of Trade, Industry, Wildlife and Tourism, Botswana
National Ecotourism Strategy for Botswana

Mr. Robert Hepworth, Deputy Director, Division of Environmental Conventions, UNEP
Global Programme of Action, and the Management of Tourism Impacts on Coral Reefs

Mr. Oscar Santelices, National Director, Chile National Tourism Service
Integral Planning in Rural Areas: A Challenge to Ecotourism Destination Competitiveness

Mr. Michail Modinos, President, National Centre for Environment and Sustainable Tourism, Greece
The Development of Ecotourism in Greece

Ms. Paola Deda, Convention on Biological Diversity
The CBD International Guidelines for Activities Related to STD in Vulnerable Ecosystems

9.45 a.m. - 10.15 a.m.	Open debate
10.15 a.m. – 10.45 a.m.	Coffee Break
10.45 a.m. – 11.25 a.m.	Mrs. Odette Likikouet Bako, Minister of Tourism, Ministry of Tourism and Handicrafts, Côte d'Ivoire *Ecotourism Policy and Planning in Côte d'Ivoire*

Mr. Alton Byers, The Mountain Institute
Contemporary Ecosystem Changes in the Sagarmatha National Park, Nepal

Mr. Ferney Piou, Ministry of Tourism, Haiti
*Ecotourism Planning, on the Way of the 200 Years of
Independence in Haiti*

Mr. Henk Eggink, Ministry of Agriculture, Nature Management
and Fisheries, The Netherlands
Policy of the Netherlands on International Sustainable Tourism

Mr. Reinhard Klein, Unit Tourism, European Commission
*The European Union Activities for Sustainable Tourism: Using
Natural and Cultural Heritage in Less Frequented Areas*

11.25 a.m. – 12.00 m.	Open debate
12.00 m. – 1.30 p.m.	Lunch
1.30 p.m. – 2.00 p.m.	Moderator: Ms. Mercedes Silva, Caribbean Tourism Organization

Mrs. Drocella Mugorewera, Secretary of State in charge of
Environment Protection, Rwanda. *Ecotourism Planning.*

Mrs. Belia Contreras, "Mundo Maya" Organization, El Salvador
Ecotourism Planning Components in the Maya World

Mr. Bruno Faréniaux, Tourism Director, Ministry of Equipment,
Transports, Housing and Tourism, France. *Ecotourism in France*

Mrs. Frauke Fleisher-Dogley, Ministry of Environment,
Seychelles
*Planning of Ecotourism in a Small Island Context: A Trend or a
Challenge?*

2.00 p.m. – 2.30 p.m.	Open debate
2.30 p.m. - 3.00 p.m.	Ms. Lucila Egydio, Ministry of Environment, Brazil

*Programme for the Development of Ecotourism for the Legal
Amazon*

Mr. Pierre Diouf, Ministry of Tourism, Senegal
*Ecotourism Policy, Planning, Management and Development in
Senegal*

Dr. Ben G. Moses, High Commissioner of the United Republic
of Tanzania in Canada
*Ecotourism Development in Tanzania: The Sustainability
Challenge*

3.00 p.m. – 4.00 p.m.	Open debate
4.00 p.m. – 4.30 p.m.	Coffee break
4.30 p.m. – 5.30 p.m.	Debate and drafting of preliminary conclusions of Theme A

Theme B: Regulation of ecotourism

8.30 a.m. – 9.45 a.m.
Welcome by Moderator Ms. Megan Epler Wood, TIES

Theme B introduction by Mr. Francesc Giró, WTO/UNEP expert (20 minutes)

Ms. Jennifer Sipkens, Executive Director, Sustainable Tourism Association of Canada and Mrs. Sherry Sian Inuvialuit, Environmental and Geotechnical, Inc.
Ecotourism: Assessing the Need for Quality Control and Continual Improvement Using Canadian Standards

Mr. Jean Bédard and Mrs. Élyse Lauzon, Société Duvetnor limitée and "Le Québec Maritime"
Control and Regulation of Ecotourism (10 minutes)

Statements:

Mr. Mario Magdaleno Peralta, Normalisation and Certification Director, Tourism Secretariat, Mexico
Normalization for Tourism Activities

Mr. Peter O'Reilly, Ecotourism Association of Australia, Australia
The Secret of our Success – sharing Expertise in Ecotourism certification

Mr. Kazuo Aichi, President, Japan Ecotourism Society, Japan
Regulation of Ecotourism

Mr. Hitesh Mehta, EDSA – Edward D. Jr. and Associates, USA
A Case for International Ecolodge Certification

Mr. Youn-Taek Lee, Korea Tourism Research Institute (KTRI), Republic of Korea
Ecotourism Management Triangle: A Future Direction for International Co-operation

9.45 a.m. – 10.15 a.m.
Open debate

10.15 a.m. – 10.45 a.m.
Coffee Break

10.45 a.m. – 11.25 a.m.
Mr. Naut Kusters, European Centre for Eco & agro Tourism, The Netherlands
VISIT: Moving the European Tourism Market towards Sustainability

Mr. Marc Marengo, Ministry of Tourism & Transport, Seychelles
Regulation of Ecotourism in a Small Island Context

Mr. Oscar Iroldi, Polytechnic Centre of the "Cono Sur",
Uruguay
Fast Ecotourism Evaluations

Mr. Gordon Clifford, Consulting and Audit Canada, Federal
Government, Canada
Indicators of Sustainability in Tourism

Mrs. Rachel Wieting, EUROPARC Federation
*The European Charter for Sustainable Tourism in Protected
Areas: A Practical Tool for Implementation of the
International Guidelines for Sustainable Tourism*

11.25 a.m. – 12.00 p.m.	Open debate
12.00 p.m. – 1.30 p.m.	Lunch
1.30 p.m. – 2.00 p.m.	Moderator: Ms. Heba Aziz, Oman

Ms. Sigrid Hockamp-Mack, Federal Ministry of
Environment, Germany
*Draft International Guidelines on Sustainable Tourism in
Vulnerable Ecosystems*

Mr. Ary Sendjaja Suhandi, INDECON, Indonesia
Visitor Impact Management at Bodogol Education Centre

Mr. Ronald Sanabria, Rainforest Alliance
*Sustainable Tourism Stewardship Council – Progress Report
on the Feasibility to Create an Accreditation Body for
Sustainable Tourism Certification*

2.00 p.m. – 2.30 p.m.	Open debate
2.30 p.m. – 3.00 p.m.	Mr. Rajiv Bhartari, Wildlife Institute of India, India

Corbett Binsar Nainital (CBN) Ecotourism Initiative

Mrs. Victoria Otarola, Mr. Alejandro Reyes and Mr.
Fernando Leon, San Ignacio de Loyola University, Peru
National Programme of Sustainability Certification

Mr. Manfred Pils, International Friends of Nature, Austria
*Red Card for Tourism? 10 Principles and Challenges for a
Sustainable Tourism Development in the 21st Century*

Mgr. Piero Monni, Holy See
Ecotourism and Ethics

3.00 p.m. – 4.00 p.m.	Open debate
4.00 p.m. – 4.30 p.m.	Coffee break
4.30 p.m. – 5.30 p.m.	Debate and drafting of preliminary conclusions of Theme B

Theme C: Product development and marketing of ecotourism

8.30 a.m. – 9.45 a.m.	Welcome by Moderator, Mr John Ap, Hong Kong, SAR of the P. R. of China

Theme C introduction by Mr. Richard Denman, WTO/UNEP Expert

Mr. Celes Davar, President, Earth Rhythms Inc.
Attracting the World through the Power of Partnerships

Mr. Raymond Desjardins, Québec Society of Outdoors Establishments
Promotion in Québec's Parks

Statements:

Mr. Gede Ardika, Minister of Culture and Tourism, Indonesia
Ecotourism as a Tool for Nature and Culture conservation

Mr. Helmut Krüger, Federal Ministry of Economics and Technology, Germany
Product Development and Marketing of Ecotourism in Germany

Mrs. María Hernández, Vice-minister of Tourism, Venezuela
Ecotourism in Venezuela: Encounters, Experiences, Reflections and Proposals

Mr. Marcos Vidalon and Mr. Rafael Metaki, Casa Machiguenga, Peru

9.45 a.m. – 10.15 a.m.	Open debate
10.15 a.m. – 10.45 a.m.	Coffee Break
10.45 a.m. – 11.25 a.m.	Ms. Maria José Viñals, Polytechnic University of Valencia, Spain

Ramsar Convention Project: Tools for the Management of Sustainable Tourism in Wetlands

Mr. Costas Christ, Conservation International
Global Initiatives with Positive Implications to the Sustainability Challenge

Mr. Héctor Ceballos-Lascuráin, Programme of International Consultancy on Ecotourism (PICE), Mexico
The need for environmentally-friendly tourism facilities in protected areas: case study from Mexico

Mr. Michael Seltzer and Mr. Ben Sherman, Business Enterprises for Sustainable Travel (BEST), USA

Indian Country Tourism USA Online Directory

11.25 a.m. – 12.00 p.m.	Open debate
12.00 p.m. – 1.30 p.m.	Lunch
1.30 p.m. – 2.00 p.m.	Moderator: Prof. Don Hawkins, USA

Mr. Mathe Kasereka, Economic Operator in Tourism Sector, Democratic Republic of Congo
Ecotourism Advantages and Costs Monitoring in Democratic Republic of Congo

Mr. Jonathan B. Tourtellot, National Geographic Society, USA
Moving Ecotourism beyond its Niche

Mr. Carlos Maldonado, International Labour Organization (ILO)
Entrepreneurial Services for Tourism Development with Indigenous Communities

Mr. Frans de Man, Retour Foundation
Representing Local Interests in Tourism Marketing & Information

2.00 p.m. – 2.30 p.m.	Open debate
2.30 – p.m. – 3.00 p.m.	Ms. Jane Robertson, UNESCO, Man & Biosphere Programme

Ecotourism in the World Network of Biosphere Reserves

Ms. Bely Pires, Sao Paulo City Green Belt Biosphere Reserve, Brazil
Green Belt Tourist Cluster: A Sustainable Tourism Development Strategy

Mr. Carlo Alberto Graziani, Italian Federation of Natural Parks and Reserves, Italy
Development of ecotourism in Italy

3.00 p.m. – 4.00 p.m.	Open debate
4.00 p.m. – 4.30 p.m.	Coffee break
4.30 p.m. – 5.30 p.m.	Debate and drafting of preliminary conclusions of Theme C

Theme D: Monitoring costs and benefits of ecotourism

8.30 a.m. – 9.45 a.m.	Welcome by Moderator, Mr. Klaus Lengefeld, Germany

Theme D introduction by Mr. François Vellas, WTO/UNEP expert

Mrs. Guylaine Gill, General Director, Société touristique des autochtones du Québec and Mr. Dwayne Hounsell, President, Equipe Canada tourisme autochtone
Advantages and Disadvantages of Ecotourism for Canadian Aboriginal Societies.

Mr. Johnny Adams, Kativik Regional Government
Development in Provincial Parks in Nunavik

Statements:

Dr. Maciá Blázquez, Balearic Islands Centre of Tourism Technologies and Research, Spain
The Public Sector Role in Tourist-used Natural Spaces

Mrs. Alison Johnston, International Support for Sustainable Tourism, Canada
The Meeting of Peoples through Ecotourism: Is the Sacred for Sale?

Mrs. Nina Rao, EQUATIONS
Indigenous Peoples Interfaith Dialogue

Mr. David Diaz Benavides, Chief, Trade in Services, UNCTAD
GATS Negotiations on Trade in Services: impact on the sustainability of ecotourism

9.45 a.m. – 10.15 a.m.	Open debate
10.15 a.m. – 10.45 a.m.	Coffee Break
10.45 a.m. – 11.25 a.m.	Dr Theodros Atlabachew, Ethiopian Tourism Commission, Ethiopia

The Promotion of Small and Medium-sized Travel & Tourism Enterprises in the Least Developed Countries and their Comparative Advantages for a Sustainable Development

Dr. Luis Castelli, President, Fundación Naturaleza para el Futuro, Argentina
Natural Areas under risk, a risk for ecotourism

Mr. Nataranjan Ishwaran, UNESCO-World Heritage Centre, Chief of Natural Heritage, Mr. Harry Dgoko Susilo, Ujung kulon and komodo National Parks, Ministry of forestry and

Estate Crops, Indonesia, and Mr. Ezuma, Uganda wildlife
Authority, Bwindi impenetrable National Park, Uganda
*Engaging the Tourism Industry and Communities for
Enhanced World Heritage Site Protection*

Mr. Ravindra Corea, Sri Lanka Wildlife Conservation
Society, Sri Lanka
*How Ecotourism can be the Economic Base for the
Economically & Biologically Sustainable Management of
Biodiversity & a new Concept of Ecotourism Resort*

Ms. Penny Urquhart, Khanya: Managing Rural Change,
South Africa
*Poverty Eradication and Ecotourism: the Role of Multi-
Stakeholder Participation Processes*

11.25 a.m. – 12.00 p.m.	Open debate
12.00 p.m. – 1.30 p.m.	Lunch
1.30 p.m. – 2.00 p.m.	Moderator: Mr. Costas Christ, Conservation International

Mr. Louis Jolin, International Bureau of Social Tourism
Ecotourism Development

Mr. Guilherme Magalhaes, Brazilian Tourist Board, Brazil
Destinations of Ecotourism

Mr. Fabien Paquier and Mrs. Tiana Razafindrakoto,
Environment Support Service, Madagascar
*Community-based Ecotourism Beginnings in Madagascar:
Towards a Natural Resources Sustainable Management
Support*

Mr. Brett Jenks, Rare Center for Tropical Conservation, USA
Ecotourism as a tool for conservation

2.00 p.m. – 2.30 p.m.	Open debate
2.30 p.m. – 3.00 p.m.	Mr. Ralph Buckley, Griffith University, Australia

A global Triple-bottom-line Report Card for Ecotourism

Mr. Stephen Kalonzo Musyoka, Minister of Tourism and
Information, Kenya
Ecotourism Development in Kenya

Mr. Jovan Popesku, Centre for Responsible and Sustainable
Tourism Development, Yugoslavia
*Ecotourism – A Tool for Sustainable Tourism Development in
Serbia*

3.00 p.m. – 4.00 p.m.	Open debate

4.00 p.m. – 4.30 p.m.	Coffee break
4.30 p.m.– 5.30 p.m.	Debate and drafting of preliminary conclusions of Theme D

Wednesday, 22 May

8.15 a.m. – 10.30 a.m.

• Ministerial forum (plenary)

Moderator: Dr. Dawid de Villiers, Deputy Secretary-General, World Tourism Organization

Interventions by:

Mr. Djamel Kouidrat, Secretary-General, Ministry of Tourism & Handicrafts, Algeria

Ms. Prhyne Michael, Director General, Cyprus Tourism Organization, Cyprus

Mr. Shadik Malik, High Commission for Pakistan in Canada, Pakistan

Ms. Sallama Shaker, Ambassador of Egypt in Canada, Egypt

Mr. Nuth Nin Doeurn, Deputy Minister of Tourism, Cambodia

Mr. Angel Penciu, Secretary-General, Ministry of Tourism, Romania

Mr. Geoffrey Lipman, Special Advisor on Trade in Tourism Services, World Tourism Organization

Ing. Hugo Galli Romañach, Minister of Tourism, Paraguay

Ms. Olga Adellach, Minister of Agriculture and Environment, and Mr. Enric Dolsa, Mayor of Ordino, Andorra

Mr. Oscar Palabyab, Under-secretary of Tourism, Philippines

Mr. Mateo Estrella, Vice-minister of Tourism, Ecuador

Dr. Prathap Ramanujam, Permanent Secretary, Ministry of Tourism, Sri Lanka

Mr. Harbans Singh, Minister of Forests, Biodiversity and Transport, Madhya Pradesh, India

Mr. Gastón Lasarte, Ambassador of Uruguay in Canada, Uruguay

Mr. Eduardo Rodriguez de la Vega, Vice-Minister of Tourism, Cuba

Dr. Ken Lipenga, Minister of Tourism, Malawi

Mrs. Boma Bromillow Jack, Minister of culture and Tourism,
Nigeria

Mr. M.A. Sabur, Commercial Counsellor, Bangladesh High
Commission in Canada, Bangladesh

10.30 a.m. – 12.00 m.   • **Forum 1: The ecotourism business perspective** (in
parallel with Forum 2)

Introduction by Mr. Oliver Hillel, UNEP

Moderator: Mrs. Megan Epler Wood, TIES

Mr. Stannely Selengut, Maho Bay Camps and Resort, US
Virgin Islands

Mr. Bruce Poon Tip, G.A.P. Adventures, Canada

Raul Arias de Parra, The Canopy Tower, Panama

Mr. Babu Varghese, India

10.30 a.m. – 12.00 m.   • **Forum 2: Development cooperation for Ecotourism** (In
parallel with Forum 1)

Introduction by Mr. Eugenio Yunis, WTO

Moderator: Dr. Wolfgang Strasdas, Germany

Mr. Valentim J. Alicerces, Minister of Tourism, Angola
Political co-operation in ecotourism in Southern Africa

Ms. Sarah Timpson, Head, GEF/UNDP Small Grants
Programme

Mr. Marcel Leijzer, SNV Netherlands Organisation, The
Netherlands
Development Organisations and Sustainable Development

Mrs Damira Raeva, Swiss Association for International Co-
operation, Kyrgyzstan
*Business Promotion Sub-Project: Community based Tourism
Development in Kyrgyzstan*

Mr. Burghard Rauschelbach, GTZ, Germany
*The Pros and Cons of Regional Ecotourism Routes: The
Experience of "Ruta Verde Centroamericana", the Central
American Green Route*

Mr. Juan Luna-Kelser, Sr. Operational Specialist, Tourism
Sector, Inter-American Development Bank

12.00 p.m. – 1.30 p.m.	Lunch
1.30 p.m. – 3.00 p.m.	Reports Working Groups A and B Conclusions, recommendations and debate
3.00 p.m. – 4.30 p.m.	Reports Working Groups C and D Conclusions, recommendations and debate
4.30 p.m. – 5.00 p.m.	Coffee break
5.00 p.m. – 5.15 p.m.	**Announcements of Related Future Activities, among others:** The Bishkek Mountain Summit (Bishkek, Kyrgyzstan, November 2002) EcoAqua (Galicia, Spain, October 2002) Ecotourism Conference (Cairns, Australia, October 2002) PECC - Ecuador
5.15 p.m. – 6.00 p.m.	**Final plenary session** Presentation of Draft Québec City Declaration on Ecotourism Final comments and debate
6.00 p.m. - 6.30 p.m.	**Closing Ceremony**
6.30 p.m. – 7.00 p.m.	Cocktails
7.00 p.m. – 11.00 p.m.	Québec night reception and closing dinner